Faith With Good Reason

Finding Truth Through An Analytical Lens

Imprimatur

Nihil Obstat
Reverend John Balluff, S.T.D.
Censor Deputatus
May 4, 2017

Permission to Publish
Most Reverend Joseph M. Siegel, D.D., S.T.L.
Vicar General
Diocese of Joliet
May 8, 2017

The Nihil Obstat and Permission to Pubish are official declarations that a book is free of doctrinal and moral error. No implication is contained therein that those who have granted the Nihil Obstat and Permission to Publish agree with the content, opinions, or statements expressed. Nor do they assume any legal responsibility associated with the publication.

Faith With Good Reason

Finding Truth Through An Analytical Lens

By Ben Butera

THE HABITATION OF CHIMHAM PUBLISHING, TITUSVILLE, FL

Faith With Good Reason
Finding Truth Through An Analytical Lens

The Habitation of Chimham Publishing
2280 Alexander Drive
Titusville, FL 32796
email: hocpeditor@aol.com

ISBN:978-0-9899696-5-9

Library of Congress Control Number: 2016946280

"The split between reason and faith was the expression of one of humanity's great tragedies...It caused irreparable damage not only to religion but also to culture...Faith and reason are like two wings on which the human spirit rises to the contemplation of truth. Today we need to work for a reconciliation between faith and reason... Seeking the truth and sharing it with others is an important service to society, a service which scholars in particular are called to render...remember that reason is God's gift, a mark of the likeness to God which every man bears within himself."

– Pope John Paul II
From a 1999 address to a Polish university in Copernicus' home town.

Table of Contents

FOREWORD

Grounded in teaching of Pope Emeritus Benedict XVI, Pope Saint John Paul the Great, Pope Francis, and a generous foundation of other familiar theologians and apologists, Ben Butera walks us through the reason of faith. He shows how the modern secular language of analytical problem solving can apply as a person reasons through the truths of faith and lives them out in his or her life. Ben is a catechist, a husband, a father, a once borderline "None," a Solutions Development Manager for a global 500 company, and as such, an analyst, and he is a story-teller. The instructions he presents in this book are full of metaphors and analogies, in the spirit of C.S. Lewis or G.K. Chesterton, to give the reader a helm to grasp when navigating good decision-making through the lens of grace. He shows a person how to dive into mystery and how to approach objective truth in natural law and morality the same way one approaches objective truth in science or engineering.

This is a new kind of evangelization. It speaks the language of modern young adults, that of the Scientific Method. The Scientific Method is notable as a trustworthy guide for discovering new knowledge, and students grow up knowing how to apply the method in everyday life. From elementary school through college, even to terminal degrees in the sciences, students are taught about the value of hypothesis-making, observation, experimentation, and theorizing. While this approach is rigorous, this kind of thinking also has its effects on the culture. It can lead—indeed has led—to an over-reliance on science to offer answers to problems that lay beyond science. When adults raised in such a culture need a method to solve life's most challenging problems related to purpose, meaning, and destiny, they have no such tool. Or do they?

Rather than urge a different epistemology upon the reader who may be unprepared for it, Butera meets the reader of this scientific age where he or she is by showing how the analytical reasoning of empiricism can be applied to the laboratory of one's life. "Test out the truths of faith," he says in his own words. "Do what you know. It works." He does not leave the reader there though, being told logical reasoning works, for we all know that logic alone cannot guarantee a sound conclusion.

Butera then leads a reader from familiarity into the realms of new, or at least new to the reader, epistemologies and of reasoning confidently in faith. The approach is simple and effective. In often humorous ways, he reminds us that even the simple questions we try to think through are often not as simple as we assume them to be on the surface. We are analytical creatures, and that is good. It is precisely this kind of problem-solving in everyday life that "Nones," atheists, people of other faiths, and other Christians have in common with Catholics. We are united by that very human undertaking. We are all trying to figure life out, but alas, we need the vantage of faith to really get the full perspective. There is nothing to fear in faith. We are made for it!

Not to spoil the book before you even read it, but that is the charm in these pages. You will discover that you already engage in complex problem-solving, and that you can transfer those same skills to moral questions. All the million questions you will encounter through life about how to know what the right thing is to do, how to know which path to choose, how to know when to endure and when to act, how to have confidence in yourself in various situations, can be analyzed in faith. There is joy in that! Sadly, the secular message robs maturing minds of this fact and leaves people feeling unsure about this thing we call the "moral compass." Like Butera, I have been there too and it is unnerving to know that when hard times hit in life, you have no confidence that you will thrive and do good. On the contrary, through the perspective of faith and in the practice of virtues, one can find this confidence, this sound reasoning, this confidence in the truth, this deep peace and joy even amid suffering, this grace.

Pope Saint John Paul the Great's Fides et ratio has spurred so many conversations since the 1990's about how we are made for both faith and reason. One of the challenges in the new evangelization has been to mine that wisdom and present it in communicable language to the next generation. The pope's point was not that people of faith can be people of reason. His point was that the only way to be fully human is to practice both faith and reason. We need both as much as an eagle needs two wings.

Books like this show that modernity is moving past the "conflict" dialogue and into one of coherence, and we live in this exciting moment in history. What if the youth of today were as unfamiliar with the faith and science conflict myths as they are with rotary dial telephones? I think they will be. I think the Buteras of the world are leading us there. I think the days of secularism, while never gone completely, are waning among many groups of people, quiet people, the people living their lives who we never hear about in the loud bustle of the media. Being Catholic is exhilarating, a quest for truth that calls one to adventure and victory. I enthusiastically recommend this work. Ben Butera is the voice of the new evangelization.

Stacy A. Trasancos, PhD

- Author of *Particles of Faith: A Catholic Guide to Navigating Science*, Ave Maria Press & *Science Was Born of Christianity: The Teaching of Fr. Stanley L. Jaki*, The Habitation of Chimham Publishing Company

- Professor, Science in the Light of Faith-Holy Apostles College & Seminary

PREFACE

In a digital age of internet surfing, social media, texting and tweets we are getting good at looking at many different things quickly, but is it only in a shallow way? Are we becoming intellectual "surface dwellers" with ever-shortening attention spans?

Thinking means linking ideas. Making demands and assertions is one thing, but being skilled at making connections by asking and answering "why" is quite another. This is true for all of reality, both seen and unseen, for things physical as well as philosophical, and they come together eventually if you dig deep enough and keep asking "why".

When I was trained and certified to teach and use a specific process for problem solving and decision making for my job, I began to see commonalities between the rational processes I was learning and some of the reasoning of the various Catholic philosophers, apologists and theologians I was reading. If you think about analytical problem solving, it's about finding "truth" objectively, regardless of feelings, strong opinions, past experience or intuition; finding truth even when empirical evidence is lacking or impossible to obtain.

This kind of reasoning has helped me to see the clear thinking found in Catholicism and I think the ideas in this book might appeal to those who appreciate rational process, but do not appreciate Catholicism or religion in general; perhaps those who were baptized and raised Catholic, attended religious education and received the Sacraments, but had no real connection between faith and everyday life. It's also written for someone who, if faced with a survey question about religious preference, might struggle between choosing "Catholic" and "none". I believe it will resonate with those who lead with their head, making reasonable and responsible decisions about how to live and what to believe more based on certain rationales rather than emotion, someone neither gullible nor cynical; someone who does not jump to conclusions, but who advances cautiously from one step of reasoning to the next.

Through reason, the winding roads of contradiction are straightened and the rough paths of muddled thinking become smooth. Like John the Baptist crying out in the wilderness, I found that reason can prepare the way for something greater than itself, something that completes the often long and difficult journey from the head to the heart.

Reason can prepare the way for faith.

Chapter 1

Learning Stages
We Don't Know What We Don't Know

It was a pivotal question—a college questionnaire of some sort in the late 80's or early 90's; the exact setting of which is long forgotten. There were many simple questions, but one stands out in my memory as simple in its intent, but complex in actuality depending on one's disposition and how much thought would be put into it. This simple yet complex question was, "Religious preference?"

The answer would be multiple-choice in nature, just like life. In life we may be told "Your possibilities are limitless." Yet we are not infinite in our knowledge, resources or abilities, so the choices we make in life essentially end up being multiple-choice. And even if you choose not to choose, that too is part of this whole multiple-choice idea. The choice options I faced if memory serves, included; Christianity (Protestant), Christianity (non-denominational), Catholicism, Hinduism, Islam, Judaism, Buddhism, etc., etc., and finally "none." Choosing not to choose would be like choosing "none" I suppose, but I can remember my eyes shifting back and forth a bit between "Catholicism" and "none."

I was baptized and raised Catholic, but was essentially practicing the religion of "none," so I didn't know what I should pick. If one of the choices would have been "almost none," I may have selected that. I ended up picking "Catholicism" since that is what I identified with culturally. I must admit, however, that I felt a bit hypocritical making that choice knowing I lived and philosophized no differently than many atheists or agnostics were living and philosophizing.

I mentioned "none" as a religion because those who profess no specific religion do have real "beliefs." All people have a philosophy, belief system, set of values or a world view. People believe things that they can't necessarily prove, at least not empirically or via a scientific method. Yet, we can and should still explore how reasonable the base premises are for particular ways of thinking and how well they stand up when pressed under questioning. We will spend more time on this later.

My parents were born and raised in Italy, and met each other here in the U.S., where I was later born. If your parents are from Italy the odds of you being baptized and raised Catholic are generally fairly high. We went to Mass every week and they made sure my sister and I received our religious education at the local parish and completed all the Sacraments. Honestly, though, there was not much

11

connection between faith and everyday life. Since everyday life takes up most of our lifetime, it's not hard to understand how faith can be squeezed out if there is no connection between the two. I attended public schools, and although there is nothing objectively wrong with that, our youthful learning years pass quickly, and if our faith is never mentioned in an institution of daily learning, it can leave a very strong impression that faith is not essential to daily life.

After I completed confirmation, I had no further instruction in my faith and even before that time I can say that it was not the best of Catholic education. I remember my confirmation teacher explaining how there could be no such thing as Hell because a loving God could never send one of his beloved children to such a horrible place. It was later in life that I would learn an idea from C.S. Lewis about the gates of Hell actually being locked from the inside. During confirmation it made me feel conflicted and confused. My other religion teachers never taught me anything like this.

A teen stopping all faith formation around the age fourteen is almost comparable to a teen dropping out of school at the same age. How well will a drop out do in that situation, and by the same token, how well will a Catholic do in understanding, internalizing, explaining and applying their faith day to day? Judging Catholicism by what we see and hear from the average Catholic might be like judging one of Beethoven's symphonies by the way a poorly-trained child plays it, and perhaps a child that did not have the greatest music teacher, or the best support from parents and peers. Would it even be music or only a kind of noise?

Fast forwarding several years after college, I moved from Upstate New York to the Chicago area. Meeting different people I ran across some of those different philosophies, belief systems and world views. One neighbor of mine who belonged to the local Christian mega-church inquired about my religious preference. When I told her, she said that I really should not be Catholic because Catholics do and believe things that are not found in the Bible. No one had ever said anything quite like that to me before. I thought it was odd since a lot of things people do and believe are not found in the Bible and isn't it all a matter of interpretation anyway? She offered to put me in touch with someone who could explain more, but I politely declined.

Around the same time a co-worker said to me, "I used to be Catholic, but then I read the Bible." Again I felt perplexed by the statement, but offered no reply because to me these kinds of comments about religion were only opinions. It didn't matter whether it came from an Evangelical Christian or a Catholic Christian...because in the end it all boils down to opinion, right?

Another world view that cannot be proven empirically is Atheism. I've heard comments like, "You still believe in God? Do you still believe in the Tooth Fairy?" I also heard one explanation that said, "Religion is where they invent a problem, then sell you on the solution to the problem that you're dumb enough to buy." I had not heard anything quite like that before either and it gave me the impression that I was being unreasonable. Somehow, though, accepting the worldview that everything ultimately comes from nothing for the purpose of nothing left me with the impression that I was being even more unreasonable.

Although I wasn't perturbed by varying belief systems, there was an underlying disturbance about my lack of ability to respond about whatever I might call *my* belief system, if I really had any. It felt like a type of darkness... and an interesting thing about darkness is that it can help you to find light. It's certainly better to light a candle than to curse the darkness, but should we be cursing the darkness in the first place? Like any mystery, darkness can be an invitation to the mind. Darkness, or a lack of knowledge, is what pushes us to seek light, or knowledge, provided that we have the right disposition.

If we can say the mind is made for knowledge then we can say it tends to move in that direction if there is nothing to stop it and darkness need not stop it, but should nudge it forward instead. Ironically, darkness actually helped me to see. Of course, being in my mid to late twenties also helped my "sight," and my ability to think in a more mature manner. The brain does not reach full maturity in terms of cognitive reasoning until the mid-twenties[1]. In other words, the difference between a twenty-year-old and a thirty-year-old is not just ten years' experience! The brain is actually, "physically" different. If you are over thirty, think of your own life in this light.

The first dark area that led to a search for light was that I really had no idea what significant distinctions there were between different types of Christian religions like Catholicism, Protestantism or any other type of Christian-ism. Since my only experience with comparisons was non-Catholic Christians casting darkness upon the Catholic position, it seemed reasonable to explore how the Catholic position might be explained by Catholic thinkers, and it wasn't very hard to find light in that area once I bothered to look.

Booklets like *Pillar of Fire Pillar of Truth* and others by Catholic Answers were effective in defending the Catholic position via both scripture and reason, but what I found most riveting were books written by former Evangelicals who became Catholic like *Born Evangelical, Born Again Catholic* by David Currie. These types of books not only defended the faith, but also turned the tables. They were able to put Protestant/Evangelical doctrines, principles and traditions on trial, so to speak, to see how well they stood up under questioning. They didn't stand up very well in my estimation.

And what was my estimation? On the surface much of Protestant/Evangelical thinking is simple, direct and therefore quite understandable at first glance. Something easily understood might be more easily accepted. It highlights something called "System 1 Thinking" meaning automatic/fast thinking. Catholic thinking is more in-depth, multifaceted and interwoven, so it can be more difficult to understand, and something more difficult to understand might be more likely to be rejected. It reveals something called "System 2 Thinking" or effortful/slow thinking. I will cover more about System 1 and System 2 Thinking in chapter four,[2] but wanted to just touch on them here. With continual probing, deliberate questioning, and slow thinking, a reversal took place for me in which the Catholic position became most reasonable and the Protestant/Evangelical position began to crumble.

Example:
Fast Thinking
The Bible says to call no man your father (Mt 23:9)
- Premise: The Bible is the Word of God
- Observation: Catholics call their priests "Father"
- Inference: Catholics go against the Word of God

Slow Thinking

The Bible says to call no man your father (Mt 23:9)
- Premise: The Bible is the Word of God
- Observation: Catholics call their priests "Father"
- More observations and more thinking
  - Mt 23:10 says to call no one your teacher (depending on the version)
  - Non-Catholic Christians will say Bible Teacher /Sunday School Teacher
  - St. Paul refers to himself as a spiritual father (1 Cor 4:14-15)
  - Jesus calls a man father, "our father Abraham" (Jn 8:53)
- Inference: Mt 23:9 is figurative language

Dealing with non-Catholic Christians is one thing, but to me, there is a larger kind of darkness that casts a larger kind of shadow. A large group of non-believers consider any religion to be basically a "fairy-tale" for adults. This is not only the strict materialist or the village atheist, but also those with the "don't know, don't care" God policy, better known as agnostics.

We can think of the Catholic Church as a great, big, giant rock in the sense that it is very visible, strong, well-defined and is very difficult to move. At the same time it can be very easy to pass by, kick and spit at. A non-Catholic Christian may seek to chip away at this or that portion of the rock in order to change its form, which will make it smaller, weaker and fragmented, but the atheist or the "don't know, don't care" person throws a dark blanket over the whole thing and it's a different kind of discussion to defend the whole rock as opposed to one piece or a few chunks. By around 2007 I had little difficulty distinguishing between Catholic thinking and some other specific types of religious thinking, but how Catholicism compared to non-religious thinking remained a source of darkness that pushed me in another direction.

About that same time I attended a men's Cursillo weekend in the Diocese of Joliet in Illinois. Cursillo is a movement within the Catholic Church that helps the essential realities of a Christian to come to life. Cursillo refers to a short course or study in Christianity, and for me it was all about those vital things Christians forget or just don't realize. After the weekend there were opportunities to stay in touch with other participants on a regular basis as part of a faith sharing group. We'd get together on a regular basis to socialize a bit, but primarily to share about how our faith was doing in areas of piety or prayer, study or faith formation and evangelization or putting faith in action. One person in particular in my group named Joe seemed to have an affinity for "study" much like myself, someone who leads with their head. Someone who, when faced with darkness, actively searches for light.

Our group got into the habit of emailing each other between meetings about things we were studying in terms of faith formation, mostly things from books about Catholic philosophy, theology with maybe a bit of metaphysics. As we found some light there was a natural desire to share it. One might say our "study-cup" was overflowing. As the emails became longer and more in-depth, Joe said to me something to the effect of, "Your stuff is pretty good. You should start a blog." I thought his stuff was better than my stuff so I said, "No, you should start a blog." and then I said "Let's both start a blog." and then I asked, "What's a blog?" He explained.

It wasn't too long after, that we started a BlogSpot on Google called *Two Catholic Men and a Blog* at 2catholicmen.blogspot.com. The general theme was and is "Faith and Reason". You may have seen those ubiquitous moving vans, *Two Men and a Truck*. The name implies a basic way to get yourself from here to there. In a similar way *Two Catholic Men and a Blog* tries to help anyone get from faith to reason or maybe from reason to faith.

A couple of years after the Cursillo weekend things changed with my job. I'm a Solutions Development Manager for a global 500 company. Since our company sometimes likes to use job titles that nobody understands, I refer to myself as a technical product manager. When a new product or system is launched, I'll be involved with the development and field testing, working with the field staff, factories and R&D. The same goes if we are testing a product modification or a factory transfer. I also publish some of the technical manuals and bulletins for the company.

Additionally, I get involved with analytical problem solving, sometimes for a single site issue, meaning one customer location, but more typically when there is a troubling trend developing at several sites around the nation. Since I was fairly good at documenting and communicating problems, distinguishing facts from assumptions and sorting relevant data from irrelevant data, I was chosen to become the program leader and instructor for a specific kind of rational process for problem solving and decision making[3].

It was during the training and certification process, and subsequent classes I taught, that I began to see some commonalities in thinking between the rational processes I was learning and some of the thinking of the various Catholic philosophers, apologists and theologians I was reading, such as the fast thinking vs. slow thinking examples already mentioned. I was often struck by how the logic process we used at work helped me to better understand areas of both faith and reason and I began to see and appreciate the clear thinking found in Catholicism. This should not be so astonishing since the end goal of analytical problem solving is to find "truth" objectively, regardless of feelings, strong opinions, past experience or even intuition.

Another example was from part of the course introduction that covered a learning process expressed in four stages that you'd be hard pressed to find in any teaching handbooks, and it can apply to any learning process[4].

Stage 1: Unconscious Incompetence – I don't know that I don't know

When my oldest daughter was six she was learning to ride a bike with no training wheels. My youngest daughter, who was three at the time, wanted to ride her big sister's bike too. She asked me to put her on the bike. She would have gladly let me push her down the driveway and she would have crashed. She did not know—that she did not know how to ride a bike.

In terms of analytical problem solving this relates to the person who has been solving technical problems for years, in their own way, not realizing that there can be a standardized process for breaking down, communicating and eventually solving problems. A way of making one's thinking "visible" and then proving that a proposed solution is the most reasonable solution.

This stage applies to our spiritual lives as well. We are all born with both a secular and spiritual eye, so to speak. In stage 1 your secular eye may be working fine, but your spiritual eye is firmly shut. Maybe you were never taught spiritual things. You can make no sense of it; you have no sense of it and you do not care. Although you are not to blame as much as one who knows, it is still a precarious situation. Falling off a bike will hurt just the same whether you know how to ride or not; whether you understand the danger or not.

Have you ever met someone that doesn't know enough to be embarrassed? This is classic unconscious incompetence.

Stage 2: Conscious Incompetence – I know that I don't know

Let's say I did send my three-year-old careening down the driveway on the bike to crash and then I asked, "Would you like to try that again?" She would now say, "No!" At that point she would know that she does not know how to ride a bike.

A technician or engineer freshly exposed to a very specific troubleshooting process will likely make a mess of it at the first attempt and think, "I don't know this; I can't do this".

Spiritually, you may know deep down you are more interested in what you want than what is right or what is true, living more for yourself than for God. Sin is essentially a refusal to let God have His way in your life and you have a sense that you're doing this. You know you fall short, but are not sure what to do about it. You know that you don't know and unfortunately, it often it takes a hard crash in life to get from stage 1 to stage 2.

Stage 3: Conscious Competence – I know, but I need to concentrate

Let's go back to my oldest daughter when she first learned to ride the bike. She could clearly ride, but had difficulty starting and stopping by herself. She had to concentrate; any crack or bump in the sidewalk would send her to the ground. Turning sharp corners and any kind of obstacle would present problems. She also did not steer very straight, often falling in the grass, but regardless, she still kept trying.

The student of rational process also begins to try, but there is difficulty knowing when and how to start the process and even when to stop and make a conclusion. There is a tendency to revert back to the old ways of doing things, drift out of the process and make mistakes. It's a struggle, but if they stay focused and keep practicing there will be progress because deep down they know what to do.

So too can be your spiritual life. You succumb to habitual sin. Even small obstacles or annoyances can throw you off the spiritual path, but you persist and keep getting back up to ride further on your journey. You strive for holiness. You know what to do, but it's a struggle and you know you need to stay focused.

Stage 4: Unconscious Competence – I just do it naturally

When my oldest daughter was learning, my oldest son had been already riding a bike for a couple of years. He was by no means perfect and could still fall when careless, however, he did not think about the mechanics of riding a bike any longer. He just hopped on and took off.

Using rational process becomes the "normal" way to think and work. It starts to happen automatically. Losing track of your assumptions about a problem, or just not being aware of them and jumping to conclusions are things of the past. Getting sidetracked by reams of irrelevant data no longer wastes your time. You're by no means perfect and could still mess-up when careless and succumb to System 1 thinking; however, it's no longer necessary to concentrate on all the mechanics of the process.

In this stage your spiritual life may become more contemplative. You know who you are and where you are going, although you can't be careless. You have an awareness of God's presence everywhere. The will is strong and the intellect is clear. Prayer requires fewer words, but more time. You take care, but as virtue grows it leaves little room for vice. The glory of God is seen in you being fully alive.

So being directly challenged about my worldview with no clear rebuttals became that invitation to the mind that eventually pushed me out of learning stage 1, landing me flat on my face into learning stage 2. Lay apologist Frank Sheed expressed my predicament about the darkness of stage 1 very well at the end of his book, *Theology for Beginners*, where he says.

"Stumbling along in the dark not even aware that it is dark, half-fed and not even hungry for more, he is in no state to show others the light or the nourishment."[5]

I think it's a perfect way to put it.

Chapter 2

Reality
Being a Real Realist

Are you a realist? I don't know about you, but I'd prefer to deal with life based on reality instead of fantasy. Whether tackling a technical problem or an aspect of faith and reason, dealing with reality comes first. Reality is the bottom line and I think most would agree on this regardless of their particular world view. Another way to put this is that "Truth" is the bottom line, but this often leads directly to discussions about truth being something relative. In contrast, I have never heard anyone say "reality" is relative, so I prefer that term.

I have heard the phrase, "perception is reality," mostly from sales and marketing professionals in and around my work. If you explore that phrase with someone and press with some hard questioning, they may agree in the end that perception is not truly reality; it only informs our response to reality.

The Two Fish

Imagine a discussion between two fish trying to reason through the reality of water.

One day two fish were conversing in the ocean. The first fish said to the other "I've learned of something astonishing that many fish in our ocean call 'water'. Apparently, this 'water' is all around us, provides everything we need and we could not exist without it." The second fish was intrigued, but skeptical and set out to learn more about this curious and remarkable thing.

After being gone sometime, he returned to report back to the first fish. He explained, "I've been all over this ocean from east to west, north to south, top to bottom and I have not seen anything that remotely resembles this water of which you speak. I've seen nothing that could possibly surround, support and sustain everything."

He continued, "During my long and tedious swim, I have spoken with many different types of fish and heard many different things about the existence of water. I have deduced from all the confusion that water is a delusion which exists only in the imagination of fish. Furthermore, belief in water evolved as a social construct from various fish cultures to help explain how we can swim, breath and live. Look, the ocean can be a scary and mysterious place with a lot of things we don't understand, so fish just made up different kinds of water a long time ago to help explain things."

"But if you don't believe in water, how can we discuss things like earth, wind and fire?" said the first fish. "What are those?" said the second fish, "More delusions? I have no more evidence of the existence of water, or earth, or wind, or fire, than I do of a giant swimming seaweed monster or 'The Fairy of the Sea'. There is no water. We would get along swimmingly if you would just forget your irrational beliefs for which you have no evidence. You're on the wrong side of history my friend." With that, the second fish swam off. The first fish was left floating there and thought, "Better to be on the wrong side of history than on the wrong side of reality."

The Two Parts

While reading various books written by various Catholic thinkers, a certain word kept popping up and grabbing my attention. That word was "reality." Reality was often spoken of in two parts, or more precisely, two aspects. There was physical reality and spiritual reality. If the term spiritual reality is met with a roll the eyes, one could just as easily say "immaterial reality" or even "non-physical reality" for convenience sake. Few would object to those latter two phrases.

In the parable of the two fish, the ocean might represent the universe, the physical world, or physical reality and "water" would be God. Water is so penetrating and all-encompassing that it is invisible to the second fish. We do not look for water in the ocean like we look for other objects. Generally, we do not say there is water in the ocean. We are more apt to say the ocean *is* water. Other things that cannot be plainly seen by the second fish like earth (dry land), wind, and fire might represent other things that we cannot detect with our senses or measure with any scientific instrument; but are in fact real. Spiritual reality is not only about angels and demons, but also things like love, morality, justice and goodness—just to name a few.

One thing we can say about physical reality is that it has certain laws like...
• Laws of motion
• Laws of matter
• Laws of energy

These laws are universal and unchangeable. Not knowing, misunderstanding or ignoring these laws will hurt our bodies. The more we learn about, understand and adapt our life to these laws the more we can live in harmony with the world around us and be happier. In a certain sense we never really break physical laws; they break us.

Gravity is an easy one for anyone to understand. Gravity pulls us down and we attune our life and safety around it. The law of gravity does not change regardless of our opinions of it or how well we understand it. It also does not change if we choose to ignore it. No matter what, it still keeps us stable on the ground. Living in harmony with the law of gravity helps us to live a joyful life. Disharmony with gravity will hurt us or even kill us.

Spiritual or immaterial reality also has certain laws like...
• Divine Law
• Moral Law
• Natural Law

These laws are also universal and unchangeable. Not knowing, misunderstanding or ignoring these laws will also hurt us. The more we learn about, understand and adapt our life to these laws the more we can live in harmony with the world around us and be happier. In a sense we never really break spiritual laws, they actually break us.

Spiritual laws also do not change regardless of our opinions about them or how well we understand them—or even if we choose to ignore them. Living in harmony with these laws allows us to live a joyful life. Disharmony with them can hurt us or even kill us.

Aside from teaching a class at work about problem solving and decision making, I'm also a religious education catechist/confirmation teacher for public school 8th graders at my local parish. Each year I have discussions with my confirmation candidates about the importance of obeying God's spiritual laws and how doing this translates to happiness in life. I ask them to imagine the following pseudo dialog between two fictitious people regarding our classroom windows up on the second floor of the school:

Person A: If I jump out that window, I will fall *up*.

Person B: No, you will fall down.

Person A: That may be true for you, but it is not true for me. I truly believe with all my heart that I will fall up; it's what my conscience tells me.

Person B: I hear what you are saying, but there is something called gravity that is not controlled by your conscience, so when you jump out that window, you will fall down.

Person A: I know about gravity too and I can see that you are very closed-minded about it, thinking it goes only one way for everyone. Gravity can move different people in different ways.

Person B: I am open-minded. My mind is open to reality and if you jump out that window you will fall down.

Person A: You need to respect the beliefs of others. Not everyone sees gravity the way you do.

Person B: I do respect you; that's why I'm telling you not to jump out of that window and please do not lead others to jump out.

Person A: You had better change your "downward" way of thinking. You and your kind are on the wrong side of history about gravity and you are dragging down the rest of us.

Person B: Better to be on the wrong side of history than on the wrong side of reality.

I once saw a television ad for a powerful self-propelled lawn mower that could climb hills. In the ad, a couple was living in a house built on a hill and everything inside the house was slanted. The couple inside was having all kinds of problems from dinner sliding off of the table, to drawers opening by themselves, to falling out of bed. But the lawn mower had no trouble cutting the grass since it could maneuver well on the hill. It was a perfectly hilarious illustration of why we build our homes in harmony with physical laws.

Suppose the couple with the slanted house went to lobby congress to change the law of gravity. Suppose the builder built many houses with the same slant. All the people together could put pressure on their elective representatives to amend the law and make gravity pull perpendicular to the angle of their homes instead of perpendicular to the earth. If the new law passes with enough votes, does the reality change?

I'll ask my confirmation students if any of them babysit small children or toddlers. Many say yes. I'll ask if they allow the children to play up on the roof. They smirk and tell me no. I always ask, "Why not? There is lots of open space on the roof and slants to run up and down on; it would be great fun!" I find it to be a good way to

24

point out how even though you might be perfectly innocent and not understand a certain law, it can still hurt you or even kill you.

How about this? There is a brilliant new scientist the likes of which the world has never seen. He is so smart that he will be able to change the law of gravity. Instead of accelerating on Earth at the constant rate of 9.8m/s/s, he'll turn it down a notch to a cozy 8.0m/s/s. The reality is that even the most brilliant scientist can never change physical laws; they might understand, explain and make connections between them all in a new and highly advanced way, but they can't actually change them.

The examples above are about losing touch with reality, which is sometimes called insanity. We can go on ad infinitum with examples like this, but is this not exactly what people do with spiritual laws. My conscience or my personal beliefs are what determines what is right or what is wrong for me. Consensus will define what is just or unjust. My knowledge controls whether or not my action is moral or immoral. If some popular ethicist or spiritual leader says something is true, it must be true.

Just as a case in point, any given pope can prove to be a unique spiritual leader. Can the current pope change some spiritual laws about faith and morals the Catholic Church proclaims, especially in the area of human sexuality? He cannot, no more than Stephen Hawking can change physical laws. He might help us to understand the laws better, but he cannot change them. No one can.

It's easy to put this way of thinking to the test. Is genocide wrong? I mean actually wrong, not wrong as an abstract concept or opinion. Wrong, like saying gravity pulls up instead of down. If yes, what would make it wrong? What is the vehicle or the trigger? If a group of animals can kill another group of animals without any moral consequence, why can't we? If we are only smart animals, we should be able to do it and do it even better.

Suppose someone said the following and really meant it from the bottom of their heart, "My conscience tells me that genocide is right." or "If I can get 51% of people to agree about killing the other 49%, that would make it moral." or "I don't understand why it would be wrong, so that makes it okay." Disagreeing with someone who would make such claims might be an understatement. You'd likely come to the disturbing realization that you are speaking to someone who has lost touch with reality. The fact is that even if every human being on Earth contracted a brain virus and woke up tomorrow morning believing genocide was right, it would still be objectively wrong. I'll ask my confirmation students if they have ever heard their parents, relatives, teachers or coaches say, "The world is going crazy!" If yes, you can bet they were referring to the spiritual side of reality as opposed to the physical side. See Figure 1.

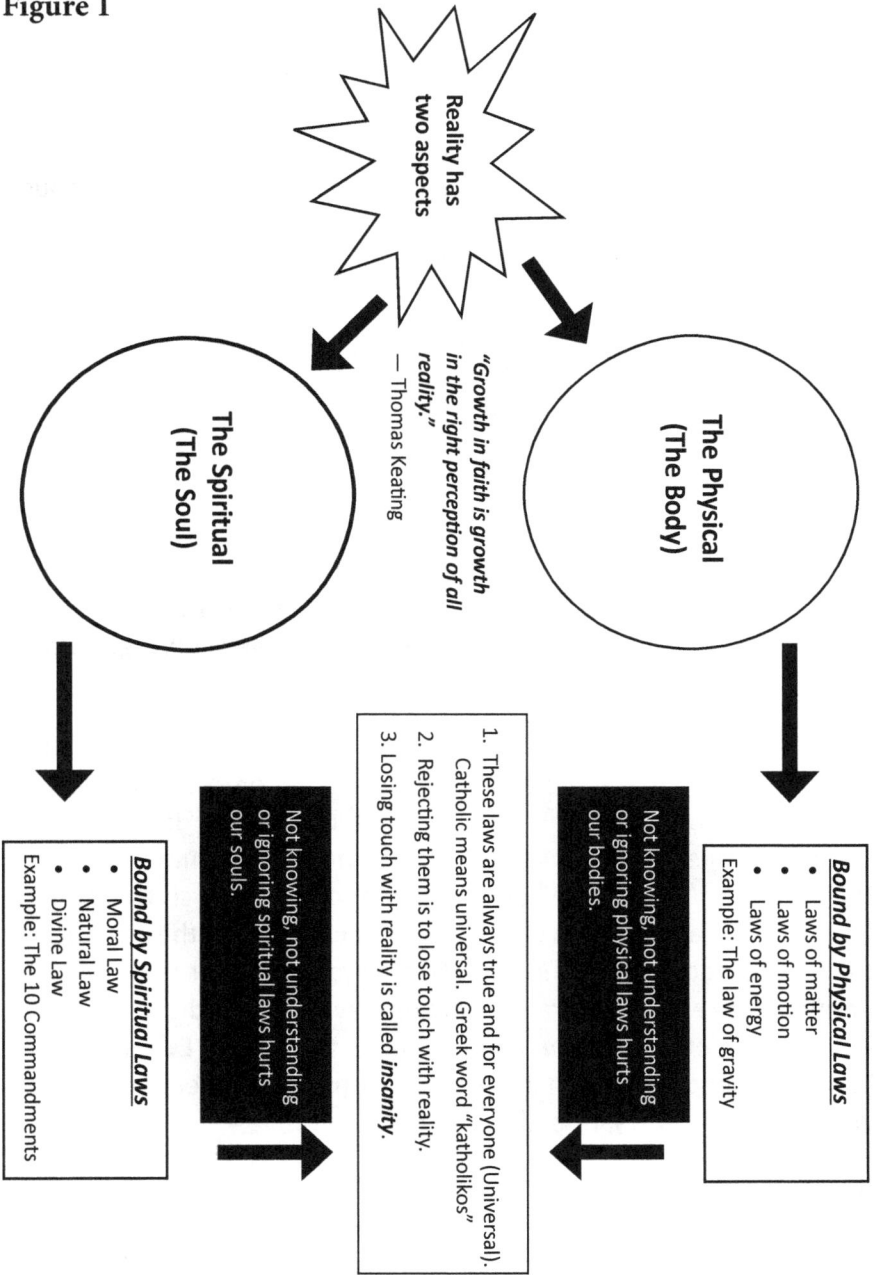

Figure 1

Reality has two aspects

"Growth in faith is growth in the right perception of all reality."
— Thomas Keating

The Spiritual (The Soul)

The Physical (The Body)

Bound by Physical Laws
- Laws of matter
- Laws of motion
- Laws of energy

Example: The law of gravity

Not knowing, not understanding or ignoring physical laws hurts our bodies.

1. These laws are always true and for everyone (Universal). Catholic means universal. Greek word "katholikos"

2. Rejecting them is to lose touch with reality.

3. Losing touch with reality is called *insanity*.

Not knowing, not understanding or ignoring spiritual laws hurts our souls.

Bound by Spiritual Laws
- Moral Law
- Natural Law
- Divine Law

Example: The 10 Commandments

The Weak Eye[6]

So what could account for such madness? To use a vision allegory we can say that everyone has two eyes. There are also "two eyes" when looking at life; a secular eye and a spiritual eye. Our secular eye can refer to not only our bodily senses like sight, hearing, touch, smell and taste, but also all the practical worldly things we study and learn about to help us function in our communities, homes, and jobs. This eye is focused on physical reality and worldliness. The spiritual eye is about how we all contemplate things like the Good, the Beautiful, the True and the meaning behind it all. This eye is focused on spiritual reality. Many Catholics end up with a weak spiritual eye simply because they don't know or exercise their faith.

What happens if we have one weak eye? There is lack of focus; we cannot see reality clearly. This can explain how those who are highly trained and educated in secular things can lack spiritual common sense. We can even be educated out of our faith as the secular eye gets stronger and stronger, while the spiritual eye is ignored and grows weaker and weaker. No exercise.

Once we find that reality seems unclear, what can we do? We can either close the weak eye and forget it entirely or exercise it and build its strength. But how? Think of a child that has "lazy eye," a condition called amblyopia[7]. The doctor might recommend that their good or "strong eye" be patched or covered up so that the weaker one can have the opportunity to catch up. If this isn't done, there is a good chance one eye will always be weaker than the other eye. As a result, the brain favors one eye, usually due to the poor vision in the other. The weaker eye tends to wander. Eventually, the brain may ignore the signals received from the weaker eye. One eye will always be blurry, one always sharp.

It's the same thing in the spiritual life; Mass, prayer, fasting and other disciplines of self-denial is a way to temporarily cover our secular eye, which gives the spiritual eye the opportunity for exercise. If we don't, we will favor the secular eye due to poor vision in the other spiritual eye. The weaker eye will tend to wander. Eventually, you may ignore the signals received from the weaker eye. One eye will always be blurry, one always sharp.

We cannot afford to have a blurry spiritual eye. Unfortunately, too many of us just opt to close the weak eye because this is the easiest way to maintain some focus, the path of least resistance, the wide road. Closing one eye will cost us our depth perception, but what are we to do? Exercise can be so hard and we can be so lazy!

Depth Perception

To a materialist, science is the limit of what can be seen by any of our "eyes." This is the kind of wrong-headed thinking symbolized by having our spiritual eye sealed shut causing a loss of depth perception. In this two-dimensional world where reality can only be physical; things like love, morality, justice and goodness are not like physical laws. They are only as real as human concepts, which evolve over time. They are social constructs, feelings, or just plain opinions. The secular eye, while very powerful for our street-smarts and understanding the physical universe, is not sufficient to understand what it cannot see and what it cannot see are the most important things of all.

There are certain things about the human condition that science cannot answer. One atheistic-minded person once tried to correct me by saying "that science cannot answer *yet*", with strong emphasis on the word "yet." I responded that there are certain questions that science will *never* answer, with strong emphasis on the word "never." Why would I want to emphasize the word "never?" We all know how quickly science has advanced in answering many questions about our world. Why can it not continue to advance and eventually answer all questions? It's because science is simply the wrong tool for dealing with certain realities.

Imagine trying to measure time with a meter stick! It's simply the wrong tool. No matter how advanced the meter stick becomes or how skilled the person measuring is, it will *never* act like a clock or a stopwatch and measure time. If it does, then we are no longer dealing with just a meter stick. Similarly, when science tries to answer questions like: "What's the best way to live?"; or "Why are we here?"; or "How can we know what's true?" or even a question like, "What are the limits of science?" it ceases to be just science and begins a slow creep into philosophy and other modes of reasoning.

The Nothing of the Gaps

Denying that science can eventually answer all questions may spill over into a conversation about "The God of the Gaps." Occasionally a Christian, or any deist, may imprudently use gaps in scientific knowledge as evidence for God's existence. I can remember watching a comedian mocking believers by using a childish voice to answer "God did it!" to some ultimate questions of science. What caused the Big Bang? God did it! How can a spontaneous "Big Bang" give us a highly fine-tuned and intelligible universe? God did it! How can ordered, but dead matter and energy become alive? God did it! How can something alive become something self-aware? God did it!

As science closes gaps between what we know and what we don't know about the material world, will the god that lives in those gaps eventually be squeezed out of the minds of people? For every gap science closes several more gaps open up because we can always ask a question that is asked during analytical problem solving, "What caused the cause?" But whatever the gaps are is the more rational and intelligent answer to say "nothing did it?"

Any thinking Christian will, of course, acknowledge the many secondary causes that exist in all of reality, but God as the *first* cause of all things material and immaterial or visible and invisible is a non-negotiable dogma. Likewise, a strict materialist or strong atheist will recognize secondary causes, but do they not essentially defer to "nothing" as the ultimate answer to certain gaps? So we end up with "the nothing of the gaps."

Consider the gap from meaning. If we come from nothing for the purpose of nothing and are going back to nothing, what is the meaning behind it all? The answer is "nothing." One might strongly object and answer, "We make our own meaning!" Making our own meaning in life may be compared to multiplying a number by zero. No matter how huge the number, multiplying by zero always makes it zero. No matter what you achieve in life, when you decay to nothingness it becomes "zero." No matter how many future generations you help, each one is "multiplied by zero" as the universe marches on indifferently. Meaning is received, not made. Professor Joseph Ratzinger, the future Pope Benedict the XVI, gives a clever analogy to self-made meaning in his book *Introduction to Christianity*. Imagine a man trying to pull himself out of a bog by his own hair. This is the absurdity of the statement, "We make our own meaning." [8]

Consider the gap from goodness. What is the ultimate source for the Good, the Beautiful and the True? Nothing. One might object and answer, "These are merely human concepts, so the ultimate source is human." And what is the ultimate source of humans? The answer would still come back to nothing if we truly come from nothing *intelligent* and with no *intended* purpose.

Speaking of intelligence, we also have the gap from intelligence. Since the universe is highly intelligible, where did its intelligibility come from? Nothing. Atheists might gladly agree that the known universe began some 13.7 billion years ago and that every effect must have a cause, so if there was a big-bang there must also have been some sort of "big-banger." They may even go so far as to agree that whatever caused the big bang must be something outside the known universe, but no matter how much consensus there is, it seems to stop at the gap of "intelligence."

No matter how incredibly complex, harmonized and fine-tuned things are, like the universe, our planet, our minds, and our bodies their origins must be "dumb." No matter how much evidence of design there is it can only be by chance. The thinking in years past was that a highly-ordered and intelligible universe must clearly have an "intelligence" behind it. Today's "progressive" thinking is that a highly-ordered and intelligible universe must clearly come from mindlessness. One might call this having an irrational "faith" in chance. If we insist on "nothing" to fill the gaps for the most important questions in life, then the effect of original sin that dims the intellect is easy to see.

A Common "Common Sense"

However closed our spiritual eye may be, there still seems to be some of that spiritual common sense that is part of the human condition. What could suggest the presence of spiritual common sense? Imagine some children skipping rope or playing ball. They will have some sense of the physical laws involved that are universal and predictable. They may know nothing whatsoever about physics and might never use a term like "physical laws", but somehow they seem to be able to sense a very real and commanding presence.

The same children or any of us really, can sense spiritual laws although we may have never studied ethics, philosophy or theology. An abused child that has reached the age of reason will sense that what has happened to him or her was actually wrong. This would not just be an abstract concept or opinion and chances are, he or she may have had no way to verbalize it. Consider too a sense of justice. It was around the age of four or five that our children began to speak to me and my wife on the topic of "fairness." Naturally, the normal emphasis would be on the things they deemed unfair, but nevertheless, they had a sense of justice as an objective reality. We sense that we are more than just the sum of our parts and whatever that "more" is—it is *real* and should be treated fairly.

Is there any way to prove spiritual realities? Some will say yes and some will say no, but really try to ponder if there is any way to prove physical realities. It can be argued that we can't truly prove anything at all. Suppose you were told that your brain is actually in a vat of goo right now and a mad scientist has found a way to input the correct electrochemical impulses into your brain that would simulate the physical world precisely. You think you are reading the words on this page right now, but it is actually the mad scientist inputting the data—similar to the concept in the 1999 movie *The Matrix*. This might sound irrational, but you would simply have no way of proving that this artificial reality is false. If all the physical data you have is literally only virtual data being continuously streamed into your brain, you would have no outside system to use as a relevant basis of comparison.

If you were to encounter groups of people who say that physical reality is not real, you'll possibly make note that they are not living as if they actually believe what they claim (if they are sane). Would they simply ignore the people and objects around them since they are all only illusions anyway? Would they walk around nude in public on a hot day? Not likely. In a similar way you'll likely note that those who claim that spiritual or immaterial reality is not real, don't live that way, which also implies they don't really believe it. They actually do accept certain immaterial realities that are universal and unchangeable just like physical laws (again, if they are sane).

How can we know this? What can we observe? What do they teach their children and other young people? That right and wrong don't actually exist? If we ask a simple question like, "Is racism wrong?" or "Is rape wrong?" would they answer that it's not right or wrong; it just is? Consider the belief system that says whatever you do is okay as long as you do not violate the rights of others. Is this spoken of as only an opinion or as universally true for all and unchangeable? Although many may claim that *no one* should *ever* impose their personal beliefs on others, don't our laws in fact "impose" certain beliefs about right and wrong on others?

Here is one to really think about. Are all people created equal with inalienable rights? Should all people be treated equally? If I can show empirically how some humans are superior to others in all the ways science can measure, is this not clear empirical evidence that some people are superior to others? If your neighbor is stronger and faster than you in every measurable way, has a higher IQ in every kind of IQ test, has more assets, more friends, more people who say they love and respect him, how could anyone possibly say he is not a superior human being? What evidence would you have to prove otherwise? So if we can prove empirically that we are not equal, what is the rational basis for saying all people should be treated equally if not grounded in some immaterial reality? For example, your neighbor makes more money, pays more taxes and has a higher IQ than you. Should that person's vote in an election count more than your vote does? Does this not make perfect sense based on the empirical evidence?

It seems, deep down, we all know spiritual realities like moral laws or inalienable rights exist, but many have trouble admitting it because it points to so much more. We also sense that we need to live harmoniously with these laws in order to be happy, so it is vital that we strive to know what they really are and where they really come from.

"Religion and science are opposed, but only in the same sense as that in which my thumb and forefinger are opposed - and between the two, one can grasp everything."

– Sir William Bragg[9]

Chapter 3

The Outside System
How We Judge Reality

Immaterial realities that are universal and unchangeable reasonably suggest a kind of outside system; outside, meaning not dependent upon man-made concepts or opinions, which is very much like physical laws.

The previous chapter talks about your brain in a vat of goo. Recall our mad scientist who has found a way to input electrochemical impulses into your brain. If he or she could perfectly simulate the physical world using only these electrochemical impulses, you would simply have no way to prove that this artificial reality is not real. As mentioned earlier, if all the data you have is only virtual data being continuously streamed into your brain, you would have no applicable way to judge what reality is; in other words you would have no outside system to refer back to. A similar discussion can be had for all of mankind and our knowledge of what is right and what is wrong in terms of human behavior. Without some kind of outside system to refer to we struggle for a relevant basis of comparison.

You'll Have That

One of the very first principles of analytical problem solving or any discussion is to be as clear as possible on "meaning". If one were to say X is not working right or Y is acting funny, the specific meaning of "not working right" or "acting funny" must be separated, and then clarified. We separate to see if there is actually more than one issue being lumped together as if it were one, and we clarify to get the most specific meaning possible. This requires a dynamic back and forth communication between the information source (the person with the problem) and the information gatherer (the problem solver). A one-time static communication almost never works out well. Once a seemingly complex problem is separated and clarified into manageable items, you can ask a simple question that will lead you to the root of things for a specific matter. Ask yourself "What's the trigger?" In other words, what are you experiencing that tells you there is a problem?

The products and systems we deal with where I work will not be familiar to the average reader, so some everyday examples will be used to help illustrate. You should know, we don't literally ask our clients "What's the trigger?", but the spirit of this type of questioning eventually lets us know the trigger, or rather, what was *actually* experienced that informed the client that there was a problem.

- Someone says, "I have a problem. My car is out of alignment."

  Question: What's the trigger? What are you experiencing that tells you your car is out of alignment?

  Answer: While driving, the car pulls to the left.

There are different things that can cause a car to pull to one side, like low tire pressure on one side for example. Being "out of alignment" is actually a leap in thinking, which could be true or false. You've heard of jumping to conclusions; where I work, this would be called a "jump-to-cause."

- Someone says, "I have a burned-out light bulb."

  Question: What's the trigger? What are you experiencing that tells you there is a burned out light bulb?

  Answer: I turn on the light switch and there is no light.

There are different things that can cause a light not to turn on other than a burnt bulb. A burnt out bulb is another assumption or jump-to-cause.

Once clear about the complaint, we need to determine if there is actually a deviation. What does this mean? The products or systems we sell and support will have variation. We call this natural or normal variation, so we need to be very clear about what is normal variation vs. abnormal variation; what is a conformance vs. a non-conformance, and how this relates to what a customer is complaining about. How is the product or system actually performing vs. how it *should* be performing? The "should" performance is determined by what I'm calling an outside system, like historical manufacturing control limits or established industry standards. These are outside systems, meaning they exist outside the mind of both a particular customer and a particular troubleshooter.

I used to manage our company's Technical Response Center, which was a team of highly skilled and specialized technicians that were very experienced at assisting clients with troubleshooting over the phone. A team of about eight people would handle anywhere from 1,000 to 1,700 trouble calls per month. Occasionally, there would be a call where the client was complaining about an observed variation that was "normal," and the phone technician would have the difficult task of informing the client that what they are experiencing is to be expected for that particular product or system. The reason for the confusion was often as simple as the salesmen not fully explaining the capabilities of the system the customer purchased.

Imagine someone complaining about the HVAC system of a building saying that sometimes the building is too hot and sometimes too cold. Of course, the performance of the system depends on many factors such as the size of the building and how well it is insulated. After questioning the client about the specific meaning of "too hot" and "too cold," suppose you discover they are complaining about an overall temperature variation of 66 degrees to 74 degrees while the thermostat is set to 70 degrees Farenheit. This is the variation for every corner of building and for all the on/off cycling time. The only way one would know the normal temperature variation for this specific system in this specific environment is via some predetermined outside system.

The perception of color is another good example (see Figure 2). I work for an imaging company and complaints in and around color are not unusual. The meaning of "too red" or "too blue" must be clarified. What is "right" for a color to be and what is "wrong"? For these cases we are completely reliant upon an outside system for color. We might refer to something called "CIELAB Color Space" to define color and something called "Delta E" to define what is normal vs. abnormal for color variation. In the case of the HVAC system or the color variation issue, the outside systems used to make judgments about right and wrong ultimately fall back on the universal and unchangeable laws of physics.

The gray patches on both sides are identical. They appear different because of the surroundings. A consensus among observers may say that one side is darker than the other, but an "outside system" of color density measurement would prove otherwise.

Figure 2

Created using 3 shades of black: White boxes =0%, Grey = 33% and Black = 100%

There is a long running joke just between the technicians and engineers I work with that is never repeated in front of customers or upper management. Whenever a complaint comes in about an observed "normal" variation, the inside joke is to say "Yup, you'll have that!"

Sports and Outside Systems

Another analogy I like to use to drive this point home revolves around sports. Let's take basketball for instance; it has rules and officials. There are boundaries on the court as well. Does all this take the fun out of basketball? No, the rules, officials and bound-aries make the game of basketball possible and make it exciting. They are all outside systems, which exist as a reality of basketball completely independent of the basketball players on the court. The players never make up the rules as they play; they were already set in place long before they started the game. Without these realities, no basketball player could ever fulfill his or her destiny as a basket-ball player. It's the same thing with moral law, natural law or divine law. They make us free to find our destiny as human beings.

Spiritual laws are not meant to take the fun out of life; they are really laws of love and the boundaries should feel more like an embrace. The Good Shepherd tells us that if we live within these boundaries, He can protect us, guide us and love us. Whereas, when we go outside of this embrace, He can't promise us these things. When we sin, we refuse God's embrace in our life and are left wondering why we feel abandoned, depressed, prayers not answered, etc...

The Strict Materialist

For a strict materialist, spiritual laws cannot exist as an outside system like physical laws do, and they cannot be outside the human mind. Things like morality, justice and goodness can only exist as concepts that evolve over time and different people have different concepts about how the world ought to be. With this logic of moral relativism it is difficult to grasp the most important parts of reality just like one cannot physically grasp a football without an opposing thumb. Our concepts of right versus wrong or good versus bad are tied up in something that either ought to be or ought not to be. For this concept to make any sense, you actually need an "ought"!

In a world view with no spiritual reality, we may say that groups like ISIS or Nazis have a certain concept of how the world ought to be that is likely different than yours or mine or Mother Teresa's. Their concept cannot be objectively wrong because there is nothing to make it wrong (no outside system.) A strict materialist or atheist should have no problem with the existence of physical laws, but if spiritual laws fall in the category of "delusion", the following logic should flow nicely:

1. Spiritual laws (moral law/natural law/divine law) are man-made "concepts".

2. Concepts are like opinions; thoughts in the mind.

3. Thoughts in the mind are electrochemical impulses that have evolved over millions of years to help us survive.

4. The electrochemical impulses in one person's brain can be different than another's. Not good or evil, just different.

5. There is nothing outside the human mind to judge what is moral or not; no "outside system".

6. Therefore, there can be no objective morality whatsoever that applies to everyone.

I honestly did not plan for this to point out six points, but the number six is always interesting from a biblical perspective.

The Moral Compass

If a man is born upside-down, can he know which way is right side up without an outside system? A compass points north because an outside system, the Earth's magnetic field, makes it point north and there is only one north, not many "norths". It does not matter what direction a group of travelers believes is north because the magnetic field is completely independent of the minds of the travelers. The reader may note that there is a thing called true North and a thing called magnetic North, but for the sake of this discussion let's say there is only "true" North.

What happens if a large group of interdependent travelers refuse to use the compass? They will eventually go "somewhere" based on their beliefs and experience about traveling. They may split up into smaller groups, but even the smaller groups need to decide what to do. The strongest will rule in time, whether by physical force or via other kinds of peer-pressure, coaxing or bullying. It's the same in societies. Even for the most stubborn and independent of individuals, the strongest will rule eventually, whether it's a dictator by physical force or just a majority via laws and lawyers.

If we convince ourselves that spiritual laws do not really exist, we will live life on our own terms as much as we can get away with. This means we cease to be truly free and alive, which is how we "ought" to be. We become small souls, locked in the prison of our ego and victims of the great lie of relativism.

The Logic of Moral Relativism[10]

If an act's moral goodness or badness depends upon the perspective of the people involved, there is no absolute truth. If this is indeed the claim, it is easily refuted as this claim itself is an absolute statement. I do suspect that those with a softer line in this respect, in order to avoid this embarrassing conundrum, might say "There may be absolute moral truth, but we may or may not know what it is."

One argument in favor of moral relativism is that one culture may consider an act to be good and another culture may consider it to be bad. The argument might go like this:

1. If an act is "good" for one culture...
2. And the same act is "bad" for another culture...
3. The act's moral value is relative to the culture...

The premises of this argument can be shown empirically by looking at two cultures that have different values about a particular act. For example, cannibalism can be considered good and bad among different cultures.

Let's look more closely at those premises. Premise 1 is "If an act is good for one culture." What makes an act good? In this case, the culture must consider it to be good. That is, the culture's opinion of this act is what makes it good or bad. Isn't this hidden premise begging the question? If the culture's opinion of what makes an act good or bad actually makes it good or bad, that is a restatement of moral relativism. The argument assumes what it is trying to prove. Here is a restatement of the argument for clarity:

1. If an act is considered good for one culture...
2. And the same act is considered bad for another culture...
3. And an act's moral value is determined by the culture... (hidden premise)
4. The act's moral value is relative to the culture

You can now see that the new, third premise is equivalent to the conclusion. This new premise is very interesting in that it implies that one should not disobey one's cultural morality. Whatever the culture considers right is, in actuality, right. In essence, relativists can never object to the law if they are to be consistent within their position. They can only be status quo conservatives and therefore moral absolutists are the only ones that can be progressive and radical! Only a moral absolutist has an "outside system" by which to judge actions and can say to someone like Adolf Hitler, "What you are doing is wrong and must be stopped!" Relativists can only say, "Different strokes for different folks! I happen to disagree, but that's all."

It's interesting how the public perception of these roles is the exact opposite of what was just outlined. Moral relativists are typically depicted as the liberal agents of change, while moral absolutists are supposed to be conservative dogmatists. We can now see that moral relativists are secretly dogmatic and moral absolutists are radical and agents of change for good in the culture! Those of us who understand that there are spiritual realities, like moral law, are the true agents of change. We also understand that the existence of moral law would reasonably imply a moral law-giver, and a moral law-giver would reasonably imply a being that is both personal and intelligent.

The Power of a Premise

Without the real "outside system" we invariably substitute our own standards, either consciously or unconsciously. There are certain premises we use to judge things, and like any good problem solving situation, it's important to drill down to the base premise or premises and try to ascertain where they come from and how reasonable they are.

When my oldest daughter was four she was obsessed with the movie *The Wizard of Oz*, watching it over and over. I often travel for work doing product testing or problem solving. One day I told my daughter that I had to go to Kansas for work and she asked me a sincere and serious question. The question was, "Will there be color?" Recall that Kansas is always in black and white in the movie. I marveled at her perfectly objective question based on a premise derived from a movie.

Another rather funny case in point is from a radio show clip I once heard in which someone called in complaining about the location of deer crossings. The conversation went something like this:

Caller: I wanted to voice my opinion on something that's been bothering me for a really long time. I've tried writing to newspaper and contacting TV stations, but nobody seems to want to stay with this, so I'm calling you guys.

Host: What's the issue?

Caller: Over the past few years, I've been involved in three separate car accidents involving deer. Each of these incidents occurred shortly after I saw a deer crossing sign on the highway. My frustration is that the Department of Transportation would allow these deer crossings to be in such high traffic areas. Why are we encouraging deer to cross at the Interstate? I don't get it; it's such a high traffic area.

Host: Are you kidding???

Caller: I understand that they are animals and they need to travel across the streets occasionally to survive and just to find food, but it seems so irresponsible of us to allow these deer crossings to be in areas where these deer are so likely to be struck by oncoming traffic. Don't you agree? You'd think that they would put deer crossings maybe in smaller towns, maybe doing it at a school crossing. It would be a safer place for them to cross.

Radio Host: You know that deer crossings aren't telling deer that it's safe to cross there; it's just more of like an alert for drivers so they know it's like a high deer population.

Caller: The government put the deer crossings there; they can direct the deer population anywhere they want to by moving that deer crossing sign. Why in the world would they place it on the highway or the Interstate? There are so many other places I can think of than putting the deer crossing signs on busy highways or Interstates.

Radio Host: You seem to think that the deer are somehow attracted to the deer crossing sign.

Caller: Well, the deer crossing sign is there to allow the deer to know that's where they need to cross.

Radio Host: Right. And all these car accidents you had involving deer were after you saw a deer crossing sign?

Caller: Exactly. I'm trying to watch out for the deer, but I mean the speed limit is 55, 65, how am I supposed to, you know, you can't brake really quick, you know, if a deer is crossing in that deer cross-ing area.

Radio Host: So you would like to see these signs move somewhere safer?

Caller: We can move them to lower traffic areas, somewhere where the speed limit is a lot slower.

Radio Host: You say you've tried to contact quite a few people about this?

Caller: Right. I wrote at least three or four letters.

Radio Host: We'll spread the word, okay. We'll try to raise some awareness for this issue.

Caller: Thank you. We need to move those deer crossing signs.

The premise at work in all this is that the government can control where the deer go. If this were actually true, this would be a very reasonable and important conversation. As it is, the discussion is absurdly hilarious. I can think of another comical example inspired by G.K. Chesterton in his book "Orthodoxy". Imagine someone suffering from paranoia says to you, "Everyone wants to kill me." You respond, "I don't want to kill you." The person answers, "Of course you would say that to keep your evil plan a secret." There is logic there, but the premise is, well…insane.[11]

What does this have to do with faith? Someone once told me that Christianity requires faith because it could not be reasoned by the human mind, meaning they think it is literally unreasonable. I responded that what is reasonable or unreasonable in terms of faith or problem solving depends on the premises involved. If we hold the premise that there actually is an all-powerful God that it is also all-loving, then we can say that this God could become a man if He wanted to. We would say there would be no limits to His love as God or a man, even unto death, even unto death on a cross.

St. Paul reminds us about the Resurrection as a premise for our faith in 1 Corinthians 15:14 by writing "And if Christ has not been raised, then empty [too] is our preaching; empty, too, your faith." To those who claim the resurrection is a fairytale; a premise could be that those who claimed to be eye-witnesses to Jesus not only lied, but were willing to be ostracized from their Jewish community and brutally killed for that lie. Now that's some stubborn liars. If I were lying, I'd be apt to say, "Never mind, we just made it up" long before the killing were to begin.

There are a lot of Christian dogmas buried in the last two paragraphs that might seem insane to secularists, but what many of them fail to realize is that the premises *they* hold act as dogmas for *them*. For the premise that there was not only no resurrection, but no God at all, we'll need some other basic premises to work from. For example, the complexity and order of our bodies, our minds, the Earth and the entire universe ultimately coming from nothing for the purpose of nothing. More specifically, come from nothing intelligent for no intended purpose.

- From nothing comes something by its own power and direction.

- From disorder comes order by its own power and direction.

- From unconsciousness comes consciousness by its own power and direction.

- From unintelligence comes intelligence by its own power and direction.

Now there's a fairytale if I ever heard one.

The Dogma of Consent

Aside from premises about human origins that relate to physical realities, we also use premises about what is right or wrong for human behavior that relate to spiritual realities. We've all heard certain teachings that are often unquestioned and perhaps unconscious. They act as secular dogmas. For example, nothing is morally wrong as long as you don't hurt others. But what if a doctor needs to perform a medical procedure on you involving some physical pain or "hurt"? What if an emergency responder needs to damage some of your property in order to respond to an emergency? What about two sadomasochists? They must hurt each other physically in order to satisfy their depravity. The "dogma" is not really about hurting people or property, it's about consent. If what you do must affect others, it's okay as long as you have consent.

Let's work with this idea a bit beyond things that are already legal in some states like gambling, prostitution and recreational marijuana. If two parties consent to making a wager or agree to exchange drugs or sex for money, it's all perfectly moral under the dogma of consent, but what if black slaves in America consented after the Civil War?

Life for African-Americans in the South after the Emancipation Proclamation was not exactly the American dream. Imagine house slaves working in a mansion for a very wealthy and kind plantation owner. What if they preferred their life as slaves to the prospect of being thrown out into the mean streets of the South to fend for themselves? They could have willfully signed a contract with the plantation owner to forfeit their freedom and remain his legal property. Under the dogma of consent, couldn't slavery be reinstituted as legal in the U.S.?

What if the Jews consented? Nazi scientists performed inhumane experiments on Jewish people against their will. What if they consented? Suppose some old or terminally-ill Jews agreed that the experiments on them could provide valuable data to help others? Suppose poor Jews were offered a large sum of money that could be given to their families after their death in an experiment. Would this not be perfectly moral under the dogma of consent?

How about suicide? This would not be about doctor-assisted suicide. Suppose a young man no longer wished to live for whatever reason, but alas, the poor guy does not have the courage to kill himself. What can be done? With consent, a friend (or stranger) could agree to shoot him in the head without any fear of reprisals.

What about marriage laws? If any consenting adults should be able to marry, then it should be any consenting adults. Three or more people should then be recognized by the state as well as any consenting relatives? If you oppose parents marrying their adult children in order to obtain state-offered marriage rights, would this make you a bigot that makes groundless distinctions simply because two persons share very similar DNA?

These are just some examples of how people will claim that moral absolutes can't really exist objectively, but then don't live that way. They actually do accept certain morals that are universal and unchangeable regardless of agreement or disagreement. It seems, deep down, we all know moral laws exist irrespective of "consent".

The Dogma of Self-Belief

What is the key to success and happiness in life? What is the most important thing? What comes first above all else? You must believe in *yourself*, right? It acts as another secular dogma. It seems to be the moral of many books, movies and TV shows. The idea makes me cringe. There is nothing wrong with self-confidence and it's important to have, but could we not write "He Believed in Himself" over the grave of every famous tyrant in history? Could we not find criminals, oppressors and terrorists today who believe in themselves? Could we not find people in insane asylums who believe in themselves?

Although he passed away some time ago, even the most resolute atheist would admit that G.K. Chesterton lives on through all his writings. Sadly, I've only read one of his books from cover to cover (so far). It was *Orthodoxy*, and it's a classic. Orthodoxy means "right teaching," which is the opposite of what we have today where we act as if there is no "right" and no "teaching," but we do find plenty of heresy or heterodoxy, which means "other teaching". Chapter II of Orthodoxy is entitled "The Maniac" and it begins with the individualistic philosophy that a person will get along fine in life if he just believes in himself.[12]

Anyone can believe in himself, and in a culture that denies objective truth, all opinions about life become equally valid, even the opinion of a maniac. In this environment basic terms cannot be defined because the definitions are relative, and having well-defined terms is a first step in logic. So reasoning with a maniac about what believing in his or herself really means, can be the catalyst for an endless game of "point-counterpoint".

If you have children you may be familiar with the game "point-counterpoint". Once, my son was bothering my oldest daughter by touching her. I said, "Stop touching her." He said, "I did not touch her." I replied, "I just saw you!" He said, "I touched her shirt, not her." Of course, my daughter just happened to be wearing the shirt he was touching. From here we could have gotten into an insane discussion or demonstration about what would constitute touching someone, but I wasn't in the mood for games. This need not be only a game for children. I'm reminded of the trouble former President Bill Clinton got into in the late 90's with a certain female intern, which caused him to say, "It depends on what the meaning of the word 'is' is." One might think it easy to be clear about such simple words as "touching" and "is", but maniacs can be proficient in the use of reason.

The above examples may seem humorous, but the consequences are no laughing matter when the maniac engages the very basics of life, family and what it means to be human. When does human life begin? Both science and faith point to the moment of conception, but the maniac will look elsewhere. What is marriage? Whatever we want it to be? If it can mean anything, then it means nothing, so we demand some kind of definition via laws, and definitions always require limits. How do we know if the limits are right or wrong? Cultural consensus becomes the infallible guarantee that all is well with whatever opinion the majority has. The underlying problem is that we demand laws, limits and morals without God. It's like demanding electricity and then denying the existence of a generator.

A clever analogy between the sun and the moon was given at the end chapter II of Orthodoxy to compare reason grounded in the proper outside system (orthodoxy) versus reason grounded in man (heterodoxy). God is our ultimate source of reason just like the sun is our ultimate source of energy. The sun provides both light and heat, but it is impossible to look at it directly. We call its shape round, but as we wince at it and try to trace out its exact shape with our eyes, we can't do it. It's too much for us. It's both shining and shapeless. Like a mystery, we can't define it perfectly. Whatever light we receive from the moon is secondary light that comes from the sun, although one might think at first glance that moonlight has nothing to do with sunlight. The moon reflects light off of a dead world and gives no warmth, but at the same time the moon is quite reasonable. Its circular shape is clear and unmistakable.[13]

So how can one finally reason with the maniac? Other than presenting the "outside system" and insisting upon well-defined terms and premises both stated and assumed, I really don't know. At times it seems to be more about casting out demons than about debating philosophies and facts. The philosophy that says, "I think, therefore I am" makes the reality of our own being dependent upon our own thinking. With this as a base premise, one could see how "believing in yourself" becomes the most important thing in the universe. St. Augustine said something that sounds similar, but might as well come from the other side of the universe; "I believe, therefore I speak."[14] The saint acknowledges that his ability to proclaim Truth ultimately comes from an outside system.

"If you argue with a madman, it is extremely probable that you will get the worst of it; for in many ways his mind moves all the quicker for not being delayed by the things that go with good judgment."[15]

– G.K. Chesterton

Chapter 4

Drilling Down
The Art of Asking Why and Making the Answers "Visible"

Every cause has an effect and every effect has a cause. This is the universal truth of cause and effect, but some effects and some causes are not relevant to a given theme. The art of questioning gives us the proper focus of attention for any particular aspect of reality. When an effect is observed or experienced we have a universal instinct to ask "why," which begins about the same time we learn to speak. Even some of the games we play as children cater to this natural impulse.

Did you ever play the "why" game growing up? It can start with almost any random statement from one person and then a second person asks "why?" using turnaround questions, which means re-asking the question based on the answer. The first person then tries their best to answer and it goes on for as long as it can be sustained. It can be fun to see where the questions take you and how far you can go until you get stuck in a kind of death loop.

Example: It's cold in the winter.

- Why is it cold?
    - The sun's rays hit the earth at a shallow angle.

- Why a shallow angle?
    - Because the northern hemisphere tilts away from the sun.

- Why does it tilt?
    - It's a law of physics.

- Why is that a law of physics?
    - I don't know.

- Why don't you know?
    - I can't know everything!

- Why can't you know everything?
    - I don't know.

- Game over (death loop—see previous "I don't know")

Toyota's Five Whys

However juvenile the above game may seem, it actually relates to one part of the problem solving methodology we use where I work.

Although I don't work for Toyota, some of what we do mirrors Toyota's Five Whys[16]. The "five" in the name represents how far one may need to dig to get to the root of a matter, but it's not always five.

Example: The vehicle will not start.
Why? - The battery is dead (first why)
Why? - The alternator is not functioning (second why)
Why? - The alternator belt is broken (third why)
Why? - The alternator belt was worn beyond its limits (fourth why)
Why? - The vehicle was not maintained per the service schedule (fifth why—root cause)

An average mechanic might stop after answering the third why and then take an effective action. Once a broken belt is observed, it can be replaced and you're back on the road. An exceptional mechanic, however, will think beyond the fix and beyond himself. He will consider outside systems. Why did the belt break? Was it the wrong kind of belt? Was it the right belt, but installed incorrectly? Did other parts of the vehicle, like the alternator pulley, cause the belt to wear prematurely? What other belts are about to break on this car?

Of course, one can continue to ask why beyond the root cause and beyond the fifth why. Why wasn't the vehicle maintained according to the service schedule? Are parts not readily available? Is it too expensive to maintain for the customer? Is the customer just lazy? These are all good questions, but in this case no more questions are needed beyond the fifth why for the mechanic to take superior action, beyond just an effective action. The maintenance question may be appropriate for the customer or maybe the design team, but no more information is needed for a mechanic to fulfill his or her duty at the highest level.

We can use this concept to help us understand why we do the things we do. People seek what is good, or at least what they think is good. As it relates to the human soul, we use our will in the pursuit of happiness or the pursuit of what is good.[17]

Example: I took my medicine.

Why? – To kill my infection (first why)
Why? – I wish to be healthy (second why)
Why? – So I can live well (third why)

Why? – Because life is good (fourth why)
Why? – Because life is from God and God is good (fifth why—the first cause)

One might answer the fifth why, "Because I like it." This makes it subjective. One can "be" alive or "be" dead. You may prefer to be alive, but life itself would not be objectively good or bad. Those contemplating suicide would say life is bad (for them). If our final answer to an ultimate question is so egocentric as to respond "because I like it", then our self-centeredness becomes self-evident.

The fifth why in this case leads away from "self" and points to something more, an outside system, an irreducible "good." Of course, one can continue to ask why. Why is God good? This is a fair question, but like the superior mechanic, no more whys are needed for a human being to take the superior answer.

Along the same vein, people also seek what is true. I can't imagine anyone in his or her right mind intentionally seeking out deception. As it relates to the human soul, we use our intellect in the pursuit of the truth.

Example: I'm traveling to Boston.
Why? – To meet a friend (first why)
Why? – To resolve a problem (second why)
Why? – To learn the truth (third why)
Why? – Because the truth is good to know (fourth why)
Why? – Because God is Truth and God is good (fifth why—the first cause)

One might answer the fifth why by saying the truth is good because that's what he or she believes or wants, but again, like the exceptional mechanic that thinks beyond the fix, we should think beyond ourselves. What would make the truth objectively good? If lies made you happy, would that make lies good for you?

In our digital age of surfing, texting and tweets, we are getting good at looking at many different things quickly, but in a superficial way. We are becoming "surface dwellers." When we do try and dive down into the whys, it might sometimes resemble the childish and unsystematic "why game" demonstrated earlier. For the ultimate questions about goodness and truth, coherent whys eventually point to something outside of ourselves; something intrinsic and transcending. We end up at some "first cause," which we call God.

Of course, we can continue to sincerely ask why because there is always food for the intellect when it comes to the mysteries of God. Maybe we should try to think of a mystery, in the theological sense, as a well of love and truth that will never run dry, instead of a thing we will never fully comprehend. Perpetual questioning, however, is not needed for a person to begin or continue their journey and finally fulfill their destiny. In fact, just like with analytical problem solving, there does come a point to close one's mind to irrelevant whys. But aren't we taught to always have an open mind? Consider that if your mind is *always* open your brain will eventually fall out. There does come a time to stop endless questioning. Few things are sadder to me than seeing a person lost in the arcane details of a problem or all the irrelevant whys; no longer able to see the big picture.

Thinking Made Visible

Drilling down with whys helps us to know where to begin with problem solving and gives us the proper focus of attention. Once a given concern is clarified down to its specific meaning and then separated out to ensure that several different concerns are not lumped together as one, we can determine if what is being experienced is in fact a deviation from normal or not. If it is, the process of gathering relevant data must begin before making any attempts at finding cause.

Consider the phrase "My car is acting funny." Acting funny can mean too many different things to too many different people. Deliberate questioning will drill down to the specifics and possibly reveal more than one issue.

- What's wrong with your car?
  - It vibrates at highway speeds
- What else?
  - It's bad on gas mileage
- What else?
  - That's it

"Acting funny" was separated and clarified in to two specific concerns; a vibration that happens at highway speed and poor gas mileage. The two concerns may or may not be related; we don't know. For now we can refer to some outside system to judge whether or not the level of vibration and the actual gas mileage number is normal or abnormal for this type of vehicle. If both are confirmed to be an actual deviation from normal, we prioritize the two problems and then begin to investigate.

Once clear on where to begin, the gathering of relevant data begins with four *areas* of questioning that actually involve about thirty specific questions or data points in and around the topics of "what," "where," "when" and "extent". We won't delve into all the excruciating details about the all specific questions, but suffice to say that without these guidelines for gathering the relevant data, it is all too easy to be misled by our assumptions, intuition and even biased thinking, especially with a complex issue that has a lot of emotional baggage attached. This relates back to the "System 1" or "fast thinking" mentioned in chapter one.

Showing how badly a person can be led astray by System 1 thinking is challenging to show using examples from my profession since most folks would not be familiar with the products or systems we deal with, but it can be shown with everyday things.

Example: A bat and a ball cost $15. The bat costs $10 more than the ball. How much is the ball?

It seems simple enough. Is the correct answer $5? You may have quickly and even subconsciously assumed that the bat must be $10, which obviously means the ball must be $5. You may have also assumed this is a relatively simple problem that goes something like this, "x + $10 = $15". But it's a bit more complex and the thinking can be made "visible" if you break it down step-by-step like this:

A bat and a ball cost $15:	Bat + Ball = $15
The bat costs $10 more than the ball:	Bat = Ball + $10
We now express the problem like this:	(Ball + $10) + Ball = $15
How much does the ball cost?:	($2.50 + $10) + $2.50 = $15

So the ball is $2.50 and the bat $12.50 for a grand total of $15.[18]

This kind of thing can get a bit frightening or confusing if your belief system gets involved and the situation becomes more complex. Suppose you are predisposed to believe in government conspiracies due to your upbringing or other factors. Perhaps your family has had a lot of bad experiences with government in general. Now suppose I were to tell you that the government has a plan to incorporate all your personal information into your cell phone number much the same way your social security number is used today. This will be done without your permission or your knowledge and over a long period of time so you won't notice. It also won't matter if you change your cell number or service provider; your personal data will automatically transfer without your knowledge. This project has started and is due to be completed by the year 2020 (or was completed in 2020 depending when you read this). Already, your age has been (or was) encoded into your cell phone number and I can prove it. I have broken the government's code.

Step 1: Take the last two digits of your cell phone number
Step 2: ×2 =
Step 3: +5 =
Step 4 ×50 =
Step 5: +1770 =
Step 6: Subtract your birth year (example: 1965) =
- You will get 4 digits.
- The first two digits will be the two cell numbers you entered.
- The next two digits will be (or was) your age on your birthday in the year 2020.

This is a rather frightening proposition, but before calling our local congressmen and senators let's employ some of the methods we might use where I work when faced with a perplexing situation. There is also a faith and reason connection in here somewhere, so here we go...

1. Identify the concern: The government is secretly invading our privacy!

2. Identify the trigger: What was actually experienced that "triggered" the above concern? It was the connection between your age and your cell number.

3. Is this normal or abnormal? We could research various privacy laws, but we'll go ahead with the base premise that this should *not* be happening.

4. Make the thinking and the data "visible": Since this is about numbers and variables, knowledge and experience with algebra can be used to simultaneously breakdown the available data and make the thinking visible.

x = last two digits of your cell #
y = your birth year
z = your age in 2020

$(2x+5)50 + 1770 - y = 100x + z$
$100x + 250 + 1770 - y = 100x + z$
$100x + 2020 - y = 100x + z$

5. Sort relevant data from irrelevant data: "$100x$" is irrelevant data because it cancels itself out in the above equation, so "x" is also irrelevant. We are left with:

$2020 - y = z$

6. Track assumptions: Is "2020" intentionally hidden in the formula in order to calculate your age in that year?

7. Verify assumptions: Use someone else's cell number and your birth year in the equation. It still works out. Change any of the given fixed numbers and it does not work. 2020 is a key number.

8. Form conclusions: The cell phone number "x" is irrelevant data in terms of your age; it can be any number. Your cell number is in the riddle to freak you out. The other numbers are a clever way to get you to calculate the year 2020.

Call any given year "g" and we are left with "g" and "y" as the only relevant data in terms of your age "z".

$g - y = z$, or
Any given year – your birth year = your age on the given year

No concern here.

What kind of faith and reason connection can we make from of this? Perhaps it's that we cannot reduce the reality around us to only surface observations, or only single ways of looking at things. This may not sound very "Catholic" on the surface, but I think it is, as long as we deal with reality in its proper context.

Much in the riddle was invisible to us in the beginning, which made it unsettling. It seems your age just "magically" appeared by itself out of some arbitrary numbers and steps, but things became visible with some time, effort and a rational approach that brought clarity and deeper understanding. The numbers in the riddle seem arbitrary, but they are far from being something born of chance. So we see that there must have been a mind behind it all, and a very clever mind at that. I did not invent the brainteaser; someone had seen something like it on the internet and shared it with me. All I did was discover and sort facts that were already there and think about what was already thought of before. In the end we found the riddle to be "intelligible," which ultimately implies "intelligence." I don't know how or why the riddler thought of this, but I do know that it requires thinking.

The same can be said about the riddle of our "being," the course of our lives, mankind as evolutionary "overkill" in terms of just surviving and reproducing, and finally about how our planet and the entire universe just happened to "magically" appear and "calculate" itself in our favor. Intellectual honesty tells us that it's all beyond what mindlessness can do for itself. As Albert Einstein once said, "The most incomprehensible thing about our universe is that it is comprehensible."[19]

Given what I do for a living, I could not resist breaking the problem down and I've found that objections to the Catholic Faith can be addressed in a similar way. Misunderstandings and misconceptions about Catholicism might be first presented as an overgeneralization that needs to be separated and clarified just like anything else, like saying my car is "acting funny." Suppose someone said that the Catholic Church is idolatrous. Idolatrous could mean different things to different people, so we might ask, "How so?" Suppose the answer you received was "Catholics worship statues!"

1. Identify the concern: Catholics worship statues!

2. Identify the trigger: What was actually experienced that "triggered" the above concern? Let's say someone observed the Pope and other Catholics kneeling in front of statues of Mary and other saints.

3. Is this normal or abnormal? This would be normal within the Catholic Christian tradition, but it may be highly abnormal in other Christian traditions.

Catholics will distinguish between the honor due to God and that due to humans. Words like adore and adoration are used to describe the reverence due to God alone. Similarly, terms like venerate, veneration and honor are used to describe the respect due to Mary and the Saints. Thus, Catholics might sometimes say, "We adore God, but we honor His Saints."

4. Make the thinking and the data "visible": Sources for the Catholic understanding of adoration, veneration and worship can be cited, such as in the Catechism of the Catholic Church (CCC), paragraph 2132.

5. Sort relevant data from irrelevant data: An objection to step 4 above might be that the Bible trumps the CCC, "You shall not make for yourself an idol or a likeness of anything in heavens above, or on the earth below, or in the waters beneath the earth; you shall not bow down before them or serve them" (Ex. 20:4-5). Of course, many forget the passages in the Bible where God *commands* the making of graven images like the cherubim (golden statues of angels) in Exodus 25:18–20 and 1 Chronicles 28:18–19. The Bible is certainly "relevant data" as far as Catholicism is concerned, but this gets us off on a tangent about authority and the proper interpretation of scripture, which is another topic entirely.

Why would anyone accept Catholic authority about anything given the sinful things done by Catholics in authority throughout history and even today? Not to be dismissive of serious matters, but this is irrelevant data in terms of the concern listed above. We should not judge the Church by those who do not follow her teachings, just as we do not judge a teacher by students who refuse to listen. I write technical manuals and teach classes where I work. If I were fired due to some scandal or wrong doing on my part, does that make what I've written and taught automatically incorrect?

6. Track assumptions: Does the person making the accusations about idolatry think that *all* kneeling is worship?

7. Verify assumptions: Although kneeling can be used as a posture in worship, not all kneeling is worship. A person might kneel before a king or queen without worshipping him or her as a god. Agreed?

8. Form conclusions: Like any honest discussion about religion, the topic can often come down to debating about an "outside system" of authority and interpretation that goes beyond human opinion.

Do Catholics worship statues? Who can proclaim this as true and by what authority?

All the World Is Not a Stage

The nature of my job is also why I normally do *not* enjoy watching magicians and illusionists. I have the urge to answer the question "Why did it happen?" using steps like the ones just mentioned. When watching an illusionist there is no opportunity to engage step number four, which is all about making things visible. The magician only allows you to see what he or she wants you to see and nothing more. This is what makes their craft possible.

Could we not compare any religious claims as something akin to what an illusionist does on stage? Would a person or group of people who make religious claims be similar to a magician who works very hard to make you see only what he wants you to see? I would say no because all the world is *not* a stage. In other words, it is possible to break down the thinking and make the data visible.

We can cut right to the chase with a formal proof for the existence of what Catholics and maybe most other Deists would call God. Remember the importance of "meaning" discussed in the beginning of the chapter. The word "God" can mean too many different things to too many different people and can be misused as an overgeneralization. To make any headway in addressing the concern, the meaning of "God" must first be separated and clarified. For some, God is the fairy in the sky and there is really nothing more to discuss. If one were to claim that God is not just one being among many like a fairy, but the ground of all being or being itself, the meaning of "the ground of all being" or "being itself" must be separated and clarified. At least part of what Catholics mean by God can be separated out as...unconditioned reality itself, which is unique, absolutely simple, unrestricted and the continuous Creator of all else that is.[20]

Proving the existence of God is not like proving the existence of a cat or a flying spaghetti monster because He cannot be observed directly. Recall the parable of the two fish in chapter two; a fish in the ocean searching for a swimming seaweed monster should use a much different approach than a fish searching for the existence of water in the same ocean. Think also of trying to prove the existence of something like "time". I can't hand you a chunk of time and say, "Here you go." Time is not observed directly. We only know time exists by its effects and other modes of thinking, but as is the case in the cell phone riddle, the thinking and the data behind each claim can be clarified further and made "visible".

A formal metaphysical proof for the existence of God can be found in a book called *New Proofs for the Existence of God* by Fr Robert Spitzer and parts of it are on-line at... *http://magisgodwiki.org/index.php?title=Metaphysical_Proofs#*

The introduction lays down the foundation for each step involving metaphysical arguments for God's existence that have been around for centuries as well as incorporating a couple of insights from twentieth century thought. The first insight takes the idea of "causation" and applies it to the whole range of causal connections. In other words all the necessary conditions needed for a given reality to exist. The second insight comes from quantum theory and relates it to the traditional notion of ontological simplicity, where simplicity basically means having fewer intrinsic or extrinsic boundaries or restrictions.

The metaphysical argument consists of five steps:
1. Proof of at least one unconditioned reality.
2. Proof that unconditioned reality itself is the simplest possible reality.
3. Proof that unconditioned reality itself is absolutely unique.
4. Proof that unconditioned reality itself is unrestricted.
5. Proof that the one Unconditioned Reality is the continuous Creator of all else that is.[21]

The five steps are quite lengthy, but even the beginning portion of proof number one, about the logical necessity of at least one unconditioned reality, shows how the thinking is separated, clarified and made visible as it was done with the numbers riddle; not via algebra, but via other means.

- First, the definitions are made clear: [22]
  A conditioned reality is any reality (like any object, particle, field, wave, structure, physical law, etc.) which is dependent upon another reality or realities for its existence or occurrence. For example, a cat is a conditioned reality because it depends on its cells for its existence. Without its cells and their specific structure, the cat could not exist. In the same way the cat's cells are also conditioned realities because they depend on molecules and the specific structures of molecules for their existence. Going further, the molecules are conditioned realities because they depend on the atoms and the atoms are dependent on the quarks and so on.

- An unconditioned reality is simply a reality which does *not* depend on *any* other reality for its existence or occurrence.

From here two possible options are postulated. In all of reality there can be either only conditioned realities, or there can be at least one unconditioned reality. Both statements cannot be false because all possible scenarios are covered by these two options. Both statements cannot be true because this would violate the logic principle of non-contradiction. Therefore, only one option can and must be true.[23] See Figure 3.

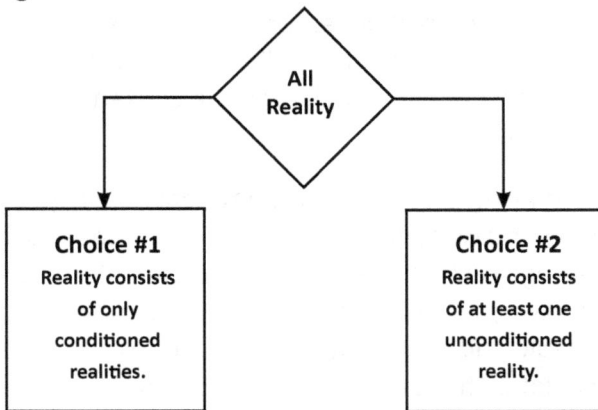

All Reality

Choice #1
Reality consists of only conditioned realities.

Choice #2
Reality consists of at least one unconditioned reality.

Figure 3

The remainder of proof one shows how choice #1 above must be false for all reality. This ends up proving that choice #2 must be true, and therefore, there must be at least one unconditioned reality in all reality. The idea is not to reproduce and study the five-step proof here, but merely to illustrate how proofs like this are evidence for the existence of what Catholics would call God. They are visible and publicly verifiable without any special appeal to theology or other religious knowledge. To reject these "data points" based on the logic one would need to separate and clarify their objection(s) and also make *their* thinking visible and publicly verifiable. To reject these "data points" because one does not like where they lead would be not only unreasonable—but also irresponsible.

A Word About Evidence

I often hear talk about no observable evidence for the existence of God. I find this intriguing because I often deal with a lack of evidence when problem solving or decision making. Regardless of how much data is available or how much data is absent, people still expect us to answer the question, "Why did it happen?" or "What should we do?"

You may think our method is only about observable evidence. It is not. Most often it is physically impossible for us obtain all the data we need or want to answer all the questions we have. In fact, I don't remember a single instance when we had *all* the evidence we wanted at our disposal. So what do we do? Do we give up and say there is no way to proceed with a decision? Do we report back to upper management that the root cause of a problem is "nothing," or the cause is "random chance," or a "spontaneous event?" No, these answers are not answers at all and they are unacceptable to explain any observed effect, including the existence of the universe or our own being.

Instead, the thinking process we use navigates the gaps between what we know and what we don't know. Part of the process involves carefully making and tracking assumptions and inferences that connect the facts we have. We then have a way to move toward what is more reasonable and step away from what is less reasonable given the available data. This is not done via experimentation, observation or trial and error because this kind of activity tends to waste company resources. It's all done "on paper" at first, using the available facts and knowledge we already have (thinking made visible). We must get buy-in that the company should spend time and money based on the conclusion we come up with, even though we have no absolute proof that it is correct. We just show how it is the most reasonable.

The main point is that at the end of the process we make a decision or determine the most probable cause of a problem. Our conclusion comes with no observable evidence that it is actually true, yet we still expect people to accept it. Why? Because accepting some things without complete proof is rational and responsible solely based on the reasoning. Rejecting those same things is irrational and irresponsible based on the same reasoning. If an engineer or technician at our company were to keep repeating, "I reject your conclusion because there is no absolute proof that it is actually true and I will continue to work as if it were not," he or she would not be employed with us for long.

Of course, the most probable cause of a deviation is ultimately proved-out to see if it is in fact the true cause. A decision will also prove itself out over time as a good or bad choice. In the spiritual life this proving-out or "moment of truth" relates to the end of our earthly life where the theological virtues of Faith and Hope are no longer needed for a soul in the presence of God. All that will remain is Love (see 1 Corinthians 13:13).

There is no question however, that reason alone is not enough, but it can start us on the adventure. Like John the Baptist, reason cries out in the wilderness to prepare the way for faith, asking questions about life like, "Why did it happen?" and, "What should we do?"

A Word About Assumptions

The assumption tracking part of the process we use that moves us toward what is more reasonable and away from what is less reasonable relates to something called Occam's razor. The more assumptions one needs to make a theory true, the more complex they are and the more unreasonable they are, the less likely the theory is actually true. Theories with fewer, simpler and more reasonable assumptions are more likely to be true, so we logically gravitate toward them. A great difficulty comes in when assumptions and facts are confused. We often use our assumptions, or intuitive leaps in thinking, as if they are actually facts and this can happen subconsciously.

I live in the Chicago area and one year in March we had an incredible warm spell. On one sunny eighty-five degree day I was driving down a familiar road when I saw a man in his front yard with some

Christmas lights. I thought to myself, "It's a bit late, but what a perfect day to take down Christmas lights." I then began to think; maybe he was not a bit late, but a lot early putting up his lights for next Christmas.

I did not actually observe him taking down any lights, but only holding the lights. Taking the lights down was an assumption or a leap in thinking on my part. Driving by, I had no way to know what he was doing or not doing with the lights. However, based on certain premises from past experience, it would be more reasonable to say the man was taking down the lights and less reasonable to say he was putting them up. Admittedly, both are within the realm of possibility. The natural tendency however, would be for me to tell others that I saw a man taking down Christmas lights when I did not actually observe that; I only assumed it.

Assumptions and intuitive thinking can easily morph into facts in our minds without us even being aware of it. When my youngest daughter was around the age of four, she kept asking me to "measure her feet". I could not figure out what she really meant. She then pointed to our digital bathroom scale. Think about it; you stand on the scale, look down, and a number pops-up over your feet...measure my feet. This is pure, unbiased observation logic with an unconscious assumption—the number on the scale must relate directly to the feet.

Don't feel bad; we need to make intuitive assumptions to survive everyday life. As I eat I assume that my food is not poisoned, although I have no evidence. As I drive through a green light, I assume the cross traffic will remain stopped, although I have no proof. After all, their red light is not directly linked to their brakes. The key is to have an awareness of our assumptions and realize that sometimes our intuition can hurt us and lead to an assumption gap. Whether consciously or subconsciously, once you make an assumption, the gap between what you think and what is reality can get further and further apart. If a rocket's trajectory is off by the slightest angle, it can end up in another universe. This applies to matters of faith as well.

Here are some examples from years ago in my own faith journey that are probably not uncommon. See if any of these ring a bell.

Who made God? God's existence would itself require an explanation, just as the existence of the universe or anything else does, right? This kind of thinking could potentially start one on the road to atheism since believers seem to be contradicting themselves. The flawed assumption is that God is a contingent being just like any other being in the universe (one thing among many). Metaphysics, however, will divide reality into two parts; conditioned reality and unconditioned reality as mentioned earlier in the chapter. The logic shows how there must be one unique unconditioned reality (one thing that requires nothing else for its own existence) and this unconditioned reality must be completely unrestricted and must sustain the existence of everything else. We call this reality "God." Since this unconditioned reality would not be contingent upon time, the word "made" in the question "Who made God?" makes no sense. The word "made" is past tense, which implies a beginning point, which implies a contingency to time. So what *can* we say with our limited human language that does make *some* sense? God just IS. God hinted at this long before any metaphysicist did by saying I am that I am (see Exodus 3:14).

What's the deal with original sin? Adam and Eve disobeyed, not me. I didn't do anything, especially as a newborn baby, so why should I have to deal with original sin? It's not fair! The assumption here is that we are entitled to salvation. We have a right to the gift of grace and eternal life with God. The following analogy I once heard helped me tremendously.

Imagine your poor father befriended a billionaire before you were born. They were such good friends that the billionaire made your dad heir to his fortune. One day your father betrayed the billionaire, so he removed him from his will, leaving him in his poverty. Years later your father met your mother and you were born. Eventually, you learned the story of friendship and betrayal between the billionaire and your father. You realize that you would have been next in line for the fortune if your father would have remained a faithful friend, so you say, "My father betrayed him, not me. I didn't do anything, so why should I have to deal with poverty. It's not fair! The fortune should still go to me." The reality is that you never had a claim to the fortune in the first place.

Next up is a common and usually subconscious assumption well illustrated by St. Augustine in his early years when he asked, "Where does evil come from?"[24] Catholics teach that God is all good and all things come from God, so we may naturally ask the question—where did evil come from? How could evil come into being at all? The incorrect assumption is that evil *has* "being." Evil actually has no substance or being, it is just the privation of good. Think of physical darkness; it has no "being." Darkness is merely the absence of light. It doesn't come from anywhere or find its source in anything; it is merely the lack of something. No one can bring darkness; one can only take away light. Similarly, no one can bring evil; one can only take away what is good.

When I first heard the titles of "Christ the King" and Mary "Queen of Heaven," I thought to myself, "Did Jesus and Mary get married and now they rule as king and queen of heaven?" The flawed assumption here is that a king and a queen are always husband and wife. In the ancient kingdom of Israel, the queen was always the mother of the king (not the wife or wives) and part of her role was to bring petitions to the king (see 1 Kings 2:13-21). If we accept the premises that the Old Testament foreshadows the New Testament, the ancient kingdom of Israel foreshadows the new kingdom of Christ, and the King of Israel foreshadows Christ the King, then it makes sense to say Mary is the Queen of Heaven. In fact, it would be strange if it were otherwise.

Here is one on Papal infallibility. How incredibly arrogant (or stupid) for an organization to declare their leader "infallible"? One would be wise to be suspicious of such a thing, right? One common assumption here is that infallible means impeccable. To be impeccable means to be without sin, error or fault and no Pope fits the bill for this. It's not about being perfect. In fact, it's really not about "being" at all. It's about teaching, teaching in the context of proper authority (ex-cathedra) on matters of faith and morals. When push comes to shove, Catholics believe that God's "decision point" on earth would not lead us astray. Think about it; if there really is a God, and He really cares about us, He would make sure we have a way to know what is true in terms of what to believe and how to behave (faith and morals). He would not leave us alone with our imperfect human intuition and flawed interpretations of His will. If infallibility were rejected, we'd end up with all kinds of teachings as numerous as they are wrong. Could you even imagine?

We seldom see things as they truly are, so we fill in these gaps with assumptions, which can cause leaps in thinking, the most harmful of which can be the subconscious ones. Even if we've got something basically right, we only see a small portion of its totality. The important thing is seeing what needs to be seen and God always provides what is needed. Going beyond just deism, when we grow in our Catholic faith, we grow in the right perception of reality, as we say in our creed, of all things visible and invisible. Catholicism is given to everyone as a universal way of seeing; a way of seeing in which we can best respond to the world around us.

"Faith devoid of reason risks becoming superstition and blind prejudice. Reason inattentive to faith risks solipsism, self-absorption, detachment from reality."[25]
– George Weigel

Chapter 5

The Mother of All Questions
How Can We Know What's True?

The action of the human intellect is "to know". We want to know things, and know things more meaningful than how much a bat and ball cost or even the way we know an answer to a clever numbers riddle. The object for our intellect is "Truth". We generally don't seek just any answers and no one wants lies. We want correct answers and there are many big questions in life. Why are we here? What's the meaning of life? What's the best way to live? How can I have lasting happiness? Are you saved? These are good questions, but I would suggest that there is one question that is the mother of them all...How can we know what's true?

Once clear and focused about a topic, there are three basic principles of reason that can apply to both problem solving and faith. After finishing *Ten Universal Principles; A Brief Philosophy of the Life Issues*, another book by Fr. Robert Spitzer, I was immediately and powerfully struck at how the first three principals mentioned were very similar in concept to some—if not most—of problem solving methodology we use at work. I was surprised, but then again not so surprised, because in the end coherent logic is coherent logic. When problem solving, we do not rely upon divine revelation, yet we still want to know, "Why did it happen?" in regard to a certain object(s) or system(s) with a deviation or multiple deviations. Other modes of thinking will also ask "Why?" but go beyond objects and deviations. Disciplines like philosophy, theology and metaphysics also ask "Why?" and can begin to tackle a question like "How can we know what's true?"

Regardless of the thinking discipline, some things are universal to any thinking process and can certainly proceed without involving any specific religion. The first three principals are the "Principles of Reason," which underscore the universality of rational thought.

The Principle of Non-Contradiction (Plato & Aristotle)
Valid opinions or theories have no internal contradictions.[26]

If I said I was a married bachelor and we were clear on the meaning of "married" and "bachelor", then a married bachelor is an internal contradiction. There would be no need for you to investigate my life to see if my claim was true or false. It would be the same situation if I said I could draw a square-shaped circle. If we are clear on the definition of these shapes, then we know that drawing a square-shaped circle is not possible. No further probing is required.

Here are some more just for fun...

- All statements are false.
  If the statement above is true, it must also be false since it too is a statement.
- Truth is unknowable.
  Is this statement true? How can we know for sure if truth is unknowable?
- Truth is relative.
  We'll need to think a little harder for this one. For this statement to be true, it must also be something relative, which by definition cannot be universally true for everyone.
- Science determines what's true (Scientism).
  The scientific method cannot be applied to this statement, so how can science prove it is true?

An awareness of contradictions can help problem solvers to hone in on potential causes without incongruities and move towards a valid solution. Suppose you came home one dark and stormy night and noticed your front porch light was out. Since the light has been on every other night, you assume the storm has caused a power outage. As you walk into the house you see the digital clock on the microwave oven lit up with the correct time as usual. Unless there is an alternate power supply for the microwave, maintaining your theory of a power outage for the entire house would be contradictory.

In terms of faith and reason, you'll find no contradictions in Catholic teaching. Once objections and over-generalizations about the faith are separated and clarified, what might appear to be a contradiction is actually not. I won't attempt to list the many misconceptions about Catholicism here, but let's ponder a few things.

The previous chapter discussed Papal Infallibility. Is it not a contradiction to say a mere human can be infallible? Once clear that infallible does not mean impeccable, and once clear about the belief that God would not lead us astray, it does stand to reason that if one accepts the existence of God, He *could* provide us with an earthy "decision point". Why wouldn't He? The next time you hear someone declare that the Pope cannot be infallible, ask him or her, "Are you infallible about that?"

How about the Deity of Christ? Is it a contradiction to say Jesus is both God and man? He's either one or the other, right? It can't be both, can it? First, we cannot put rigid definitions on God like we can with shapes like a circle or a square. Second, I think saying Christ is both God and man is no more a contradiction than saying I am both a husband and a father.

The development of doctrine can create an illusion of contradiction. If the Truth does not change, why has the Catholic Church changed or added to its teaching over the centuries. Imagine a dimly-lit room. You can barely make out the shape of the room and the faint outline of some furniture. If we turn up the lights, we see things more clearly, even the color of things, the paintings on the wall and all the knickknacks on the coffee and end tables. The room did not change—we can see it more clearly. It's the same idea with the development of doctrine. The Truth has not changed; it has just become better understood.

Do the four different gospel accounts of the life and times of Jesus and His miracles contradict each other? Consider the Resurrection as written in each gospel. All four have a different take with different details. Is this evidence that the Resurrection is a farce? I think it's exactly the opposite; it's evidence of its authenticity. From my experience, whenever I hear different people describe the same complex and puzzling situation, mixed in with some emotional baggage, the gist of the problem is the same after some deliberate questioning, but many of the details are different. In fact, I would be surprised and even suspicious if each account was *exactly* the same.

No one can be forced to accept Catholic dogmas, but they can also not be validly rejected via the principle of non-contradiction. This is not so for at least one other non-Catholic Christian dogma. Anyone who accepts the dogma of Sola Scriptura (Bible alone) runs into the wall of contradiction and most likely does not realize it. If one believes that all matters of Christian doctrine and practice should be based on the Bible alone, then one accepts a contradiction. The problem is that this doctrine is not found in the Bible (it's unbiblical), so you need some other non-biblical source of authority to declare it. If this wasn't clear enough, the Bible itself points us to another authority. In 1Timothy 3:15 the pillar and foundation of Truth is said to be the Church, not scripture itself.

Atheists and materialists can also fall prey to the principle of non-contradiction. Anything that has a beginning has a cause. In other words, some condition or set of conditions must already exist for a "thing" to begin; it's the universal law of cause and effect. Some rather intelligent people seem content to say that sometimes the cause of something is "nothing", like Stephen Hawking and Leonard Mlodinow state in their book *The Grand Design*. They tell us, "Because there is a law such as gravity, the universe can and will create itself from nothing. Spontaneous creation is the reason there is something rather than nothing, why the universe exists, why we exist."[27] When faced with a complex problem at work, there are days I wish I could tell my boss, "No point in trying to find the root cause sir. The effect we have observed spontaneously created itself from nothing." No one should accept an answer like that. From nothing only comes nothing.

Quantum physics is also cited in terms of something coming from nothing such as the case of virtual particles coming into and out of existence. This is amusing because the "nothing" is actually a quantum vacuum of non-zero energy. This does not qualify as "nothing". A quote by David Albert, Director of the M.A. Program in The Philosophical Foundations of Physics at Columbia University, puts this very well:

"The fact that some arrangements of fields happen to correspond to the existence of particles and some don't is not a whit more mysterious than the fact that some of the possible arrangements of my fingers happen to correspond to the existence of a fist and some don't. And the fact that particles can pop in and out of existence, over time, as those fields rearrange themselves, is not a whit more mysterious than the fact that fists can pop in and out of existence, over time, as my fingers rearrange themselves. And none of these poppings—if you look at them aright—amount to anything even remotely in the neighborhood of a creation from nothing."[28]

Self-contained contradictions are also used as amateur attempts to mock the existence of God. For example, "Can God make a four sided triangle?" or "Can God make a weight so heavy that He cannot lift it?" In a way contradictions are beyond not being true; they are meaning-less. They cannot be, therefore they have no "being", and therefore they are no-thing; they are nothing. If you have uttered a contradiction you have said nothing—and nothing is impossible with God.

Evil is a big topic and apparent contradiction. Many are familiar with what the Greek philosopher Epicurus said centuries ago, "Is God willing to prevent evil, but not able? Then he is not omnipotent. Is he able, but not willing? Then he is malevolent. Is he both able and willing? Then whence cometh evil? Is he neither able nor willing? Then why call him God?"

We wonder how a God that is all-powerful, all-knowing and all-loving can permit such horrific evil in our world. We conclude that there must be at least some error, weakness or indifference about God. A flawed assumption with this kind of thinking is that finite humans can fully understand perfect power, perfect knowledge and perfect love. Think of a child receiving a flu shot. Should the child conclude that the parents either do not know shots are painful, they do not have the power to stop it or that they just don't care? This is not meant to compare evil to a flu shot, but it is meant to compare the perspective of a child to our perspective of God.

Like us, St. Augustine had similar questions about evil before his conversion to Catholicism. He practiced Manichaeism in his younger days, which taught that there were two forces in the universe of equal power, one good and one evil. This would mean that God could not be all-powerful since there was a matching power of evil to counteract Him. Being the intellectual that he was, Augustine knew about Catholicism. He knew that Catholics taught that God was all-good and all things came from God. His question for Catholics was "Where does evil come from?"[29] If God is all-good and all things come from God, how could anything be evil? How could evil come into being at all?

It's simple logic, but we should remind ourselves how a bad assumption can twist simple logic. The assumption in play, as mentioned in chapter four, is that evil has "being". Catholics taught and still teach that evil has no substance or being; just like physical darkness has no being. Darkness is merely the absence of light. It doesn't find its source in anything; it is merely the lack of something. By the way, the Devil is not a source of evil, just like nighttime is not a source of darkness.

After his conversion, Augustine equated evil to "disharmony". I play some guitar and I've owned my current guitar for more than twenty years. I can hear when it is even slightly out-of-tune, even if one string has the slightest disharmony with the other five. It may sound perfectly fine to you, but I know it can sound better. In a sense, I know my guitar's perfection within the context of its nature. When all six strings are way out-of-tune, the guitar is gravely out of harmony with how it should be, and playing any chord would make an "evil" sound to anyone's ears. I've heard it said that without evil there would be no such thing as good. That is akin to saying without an out-of-tune guitar there would be no such thing as an in-tune guitar.

St. Thomas Aquinas tells us that good signifies "perfect being" and evil signifies "the privation of perfect being"[30], so when a thing lacks a perfection it ought to have, we perceive the deficiency as an evil. Blindness is evil for a human because a human ought to have sight. Blindness is not evil for a stone because a stone should not have sight. Also, think of a tree seedling trying to grow into as perfect of a tree as it can within its nature. Things preventing this like insects, disease, bad weather, animals, or a man with an axe, are evil to the tree in the sense that they bring deficiency to it.

How does any of this help anyone? Does it take away the pain and confusion when we witness the most horrifying carnage from both man and nature? So what if evil has no "being"? So what if we understand evil better? We can still ask, "Why does God allow the privation of goodness to happen?"

There are two things I've learned from years of dealing with complex problems that has helped me deal with the problem of evil. One is that the more you understand a problem, the better you can deal with it, even if you can't necessarily solve it. Secondly, the data doesn't always "fit". Even after a complex problem has been long since solved, we can look back at some of the observable facts and see that they conflicted with our solution in some way. Even so, we cannot discount all the data that *did* fit and the thinking process we used to lead us to the solution. Some data points never make good sense, but we don't throw out everything else because of them. Rejecting what Catholics call God and the ultimacy of Goodness, Beauty and Truth because of the existence of evil is somewhat like throwing out the baby with the bathwater.

"There are some who come to him through their minds, through study, and through considering the problems of today, suffering above all. We should be ready to discuss their thoughts with them, not in order to score points against them in argument, but to help them clarify their own ideas, to form their own conclusions – this, with the gentleness of Christ, that they like the disciples on the road, may feel their hearts burning within them as the mystery of the Redemption begins to shine in their minds."
– Caryll Houselander

The Principle of Objective Evidence (Plato & Aristotle)
Non-arbitrary opinions or theories are based upon publicly verifiable evidence.[32]

Data accessible only to you is subjective. Data accessible to everyone is objective. This is not to say that data only accessible to you is not true; it's just not good, objective evidence. When problem solving, this concept can be embodied in something we call a problem specification. Without going into all the details, a problem specification is a formal way of sorting relevant data from irrelevant data, documenting the specific facts and making them "visible" to everyone. Grade schools teach this basic principle to children via the activity of Show and Tell. Telling is not good enough; we must learn to "show" and show in a public way.

This may be where the materialist or atheist thinks he has the deist cornered. There is no publicly verifiable evidence for the existence of God, right? People always "tell" and never "show". Even if we exclude evidence via the historical method, witnesses of events past and present and those today who witness with their very lives, there are still many proofs for the existence of what Catholics would call God; they are also publicly verifiable and the thinking is made "visible" which we touched upon in chapter four. The reality of these proofs does not mean that all who read and understand them will have faith in God, but they are publicly verifiable evidence nonetheless.

As a side note for any Christian or Deist—if you were to say God told me "x", or The Holy Spirit told me "y", or I know "z" is true in my heart, it may all be perfectly true, but it is not good objective evidence since it is data only accessible to you.

By the way, if you ever wondered why it takes the Catholic Church so long to declare a saint a saint, it is because they are sorting relevant data from irrelevant data, looking for publicly verifiable evidence and making the thinking visible. These things take time.

A Word About History

"It is quite often forgotten that the full truth of history eludes documentary verification just as much as the truth of being escapes the experimental approach. So it must be said that historical science in the narrowest sense of the term not only reveals, but also conceals history."[33]

– Fr. Joseph Ratzinger

How can we know what's true about history? What is the reality of the past? Catholicism will make claims about the past that are not intended to be figurative, but real events, like people rising from the dead and such. In fact, the entire Christian faith hinges on the base premise of the Resurrection of Christ. If any legitimate archeologist ever claims to have found the bodily remains of Jesus, he'll make some serious headlines (more about the reasonableness or unreasonableness of the resurrection in chapter six). Until recent times (like after photography was invented), information was passed down from generation to generation by word of mouth or by writing things down. We trust in what is passed on to us with a kind of faith, but there is a way to provide publicly verifiable evidence about history; it is via the historical method.

In the scientific method a theory can be tested with experiments. The historical method can't recreate the past, but one can still gather relevant data as sources of information, such as a historian's record of events, other public records and archaeological findings. From here the evidence is critiqued in light of the question being asked or subject being examined in terms of authenticity and integrity. A formal statement of the findings is then made based on the relevant data, and a key thing to understand is that the historian is not working toward an absolute statement about what definitely happened in the past, except for inconsequential points like George Washington was born in 1732. A historian instead works to present a theory that will explain the most data, which brings us gracefully to the next principle of reason.

76

The Principle of Complete Explanation (Socrates, Plato & Aristotle)
The best opinion or theory is the one that explains the most data.[34]

When a number of *possible* causes of a problem have been identified, problem solvers are challenged to identify the best opinion or
theory as the most probable cause by looking at any assumptions
that have been made and documented. In the end one explanation
is often better than another, but how do we know what's better?
The best explanation will have the fewest number of assumptions,
the most reasonable assumptions and the overall simplest assumptions.

One day I was taking my three children to school on my way to
work. I stopped in a donut place to buy a couple of dozen donuts to
share with the members of the problem solving class I was teaching. I also picked up a 10-pack of those small donut holes for the
kids to share in the car. I told the kids they could each have two in
the car on the way to school and we would worry about the rest
later. Not long after I said to take two, my oldest son strongly ac-
cused my youngest daughter of taking three. "I saw her eat three!"
he exclaimed. My youngest daughter strongly denied it. My other
daughter was not sure what happened.

I took the 10-pack and counted four donut holes remaining, which
would make sense if each kid took two. None of my children have
a habit of lying, but for my youngest daughter to be right I must
assume that my son provided what we sometimes call "bad data".
Bad data could come from lying or just from someone thinking they
observed something that they did not, or some other misunderstanding or miscalculation. For my son to be right I must assume
that my daughter provided "bad data" *and* the donut place must
have packed eleven donuts in the 10-pack by mistake. Remember
that four donuts remained.

So for my daughter to be right I only needed one assumption to be
true.
     1. My son provided "bad data".

For my son to be right I needed two assumptions.
     1. My daughter provided "bad data".
     2. Donut place packed 11 donuts.

Which explanation has the fewest number of assumptions, the most reasonable assumptions and the overall simplest assumptions? My daughter being right best explains all the available data. This does not necessarily make it true, but it makes it the most reasonable inference. As you might imagine, arguments between my family and me at home are sometimes an interesting experience.

1,500 Years of Missing Data

Non-Catholic Christians are in the unenviable situation of trying to explain a lack of Christian data from shortly after the Book of Acts was written to around the time of the Protestant Reformation; about 1,500 years. Did the Holy Spirit abandon the Church for 1,500 years and then finally reemerge in the hearts of Martin Luther, John Calvin and others to guide them all to Truth? If so, the reformers and their descendants would surely agree on doctrine, and all non-Catholic Christians would follow their teachings today with no further divisions needed, right? Or perhaps the *real* Christians went underground to hide from the oppressive Catholic Church and were finally able to resurface after 1,500 years. If we are to follow the previous principle of reason, we should ask, "Where is the publicly verifiable evidence for the existence of this 1,500 year underground church?" What if we claimed instead that the Church Christ founded has had a lot of problems over the centuries, but has never stopped being the one universal and apostolic Church on earth and it is called the Catholic Church today? Which explanation of Christian historical data has the fewest number of assumptions, the most reasonable assumptions and the overall simplest assumptions?

The Evolutionary Magic Wand

The world view of materialism does not explain the most important "data" found in the human condition. Truth, Beauty, Goodness, Morality, Love, Justice, Purpose, etc., cannot be reduced down to only physical elements of matter and energy if they are to have any meaning. Everything about life cannot be explained by merely seeking biological opportunities, or by avoiding biological dangers without some serious gaps.

To avoid these data gaps some will simply wave the evolutionary magic wand. For instance, how can evolution explain homosexuality in terms of a species surviving and reproducing? I was once told

that having a certain homosexual percentage in the population prevents overbreeding, and thus helps the species as a whole. So there
you have it, and how can anyone argue with such a firm wave of the
evolutionary magic wand.

A book called *A Meaningful World* by Benjamin Wiker and Jonathan Witt is a brilliant read about how the arts and sciences reveal
the genius and purpose of nature as opposed to mindlessness and
purposelessness. Just about any science or nature documentary will
express a kind of "Alice in Wonderland" amazement about nature.
This often goes hand in hand with a dogma of meaninglessness,
which holds that all things in the end come from nothing intelligent
and with no intended purpose, regardless of how brilliantly it is
put together. The finely- tuned universe, our planet, and the first
life form just magically appear by themselves given enough time
for matter and energy to jostle around. Once life creates itself, it
evolves thoughtlessly into many things including us. It seems mindlessness can do things better than the human mind can. In fact,
mindlessness can explain anything if we try hard enough.

This brings us to a discussion about something called "phlogiston"
as mentioned in chapter five of the book in the context of evolution.[35] Phlogiston is the Greek word for "burn" or to "set on fire".
In the 1600's and 1700's scientists believed that things that burned
had phlogiston in them (like an element) that was released during
burning. This explained why things were lighter after burning. It also
explains why a candle would go out if placed under a glass globe.
The released phlogiston would fill the globe and eventually snuff
out the candle.

A French chemist named Antoine Lavoisier believed that phlogiston
did not exist. He showed how burning pure mercury would make
it heavier as it took on oxygen and became mercury oxide. Phlogis-
tians explained this away by saying that sometimes phlogiston had
negative weight. Lavoisier's frustration came through in this quote:

"Chemists have made phlogiston a vague principle, which is not
strictly defined and which consequently fits all explanations de-
manded of it. Sometimes it has weight, sometimes it has not; sometimes it is free fire, sometimes it is fire combined with an earth;
sometimes it passes through the pores of vessels, sometimes they
are impenetrable to it. It explains at once causticity and non-caus-

ticity, transparency and opacity, color and the absence of colors. It is veritable Proteus that changes its form every instant!"[36]

Seems the phlogiston arguments were not only bad science, but also bad problem solving. First make a conclusion and then find the facts. Facts that do not fit are explained by piling up assumptions until they do fit. In all fairness, this compares to bad religion too. If your answer to every question is, "God did it," you won't be a good evangelist. If you only quote Bible verses that fit your premise and ignore or explain away those that don't, you twist the Word of God to fit your own words and your own will. You might have heard the phrase "God is good—all the time." If God is good *only* when He agrees with you and your conclusions, then your religion has become linked to your own selfishness.

In a similar way Darwinism is used as the do-anything and do-everything explanation of life. I remember a conversation about moral conscience in context of "survival of the fittest". An example was given of someone who felt very guilty for forgetting to leave a tip at a restaurant after a good meal with good service. He felt so bad that he went all the way back to the restaurant from his home to find the server and give her the gratuity. Why? He almost never frequents that restaurant and is likely to never see the server again. Survival of the fittest can explain selfishness, but this? The answer given was that since humans live in communities, we evolved an instinct to take care of others in our tribe, which increases the chance of our own survival. This may make sense for your own community, family or "tribe", but people are helping distant strangers all the time. Sometimes natural selection explains selfishness and sometimes self-giving. Any situation can be explained via evolution if enough effort and creativity is put forth.

In another conversation, structured music was brought up as part of human culture, which makes us fundamentally different than animals. Consider our closest animal relatives; about 96% of a chimp's DNA is genetically similar to ours, but they share 0% of our music. I wouldn't necessarily expect a 96% match, but if all we essentially are is a surviving DNA code, I would expect greater than a 0% match. Whale songs and birds singing were given as the evolutionary origins that explain human music. I was left to wonder, are those really songs or just sounds that whales and birds make and it is just *we* humans who call them songs? Once again, it's hard to argue with a magic wand.

An example was given in *A Meaningful World* about finding a species of cheetah that could run 6000 mph instead of 60 mph. Natural selection in and around chasing down food would not explain such speed. We would have to look elsewhere. Similarly, human intelligence is evolutionary excess in terms of only surviving and reproducing. Monkeys survive just fine on this planet. There is no need for a species to be so much more intelligent than them, let alone a species capable of producing individuals like Newton, Einstein and Shakespeare while the rest of their kind marvel at not only their existence, but existence itself. If the universe is meaningless, we are the only species unfortunate enough to recognize it.

The Data from Design

Consider too the missing data from design. No matter how much evidence of purposeful design is found in our precisely-made universe and planet, the data is explained away by "dumb luck". Additionally, the origins of life cannot be explained by the survival of the fittest, because in the beginning there was nothing alive to survive to be the fittest. For some, the random bumping of matter and energy will have to do as the explanation. Chance is used to explain away any data which points to deliberate design. How well does randomness really explain all the data compared to an intelligent cause?

The existence of our planet is another one of those things that is not explained by surviving and reproducing. Planets have no genetic parents. We could discuss the Earth's precise position to the sun, its perfect size, the perfect size and position of the moon, the effect of other plants like Jupiter on the Earth and how the temperature on Earth is always in a narrow life supporting range. We could talk about how fire, which has been so important for mankind, can be managed in our atmosphere in a controlled burn for cooking, lighting and warmth. There is just enough oxygen in the atmosphere to easily start a fire, but imagine if there was too much oxygen. How about electricity? In our modern times imagine if electrons did not happen to behave as they do. Imagine if there was no such thing as electricity; not only no electric lights, but no electronics of any kind. We take these things for granted, but I'd like to focus some well-deserved attention onto something else we use every day. There are many things that point to the purposeful design of our planet, but none more amazing than water.

Another individual with an atheistic worldview once told me that the fine-tuning of the universe is no more remarkable than a puddle of water. We can observe that water will perfectly fit the shape of the puddle hole. No one ever asks, "What are the odds of that particular amount of water fitting that particular hole so perfectly?" I responded with something to the effect that the puddle is a conditioned reality like any other physical reality. What are the physical conditions needed for the water to fit the hole and why does it need to be that way? Why does anything need to be anyway at all? It relates to the metaphysical question of "Why something instead of nothing?" Besides being able to fit a puddle hole, water has a litany of amazing properties that no one could ever guess given only water; they are only discovered in the context of water as the liquid of life.[37]

Simplicity: Earth, wind, fire and water are not basic elements as once thought, but water is as simple and plentiful as a compound can be. This simplicity made it easy to recognize the two basic elements of hydrogen and oxygen in a simple 2:1 ratio (H_2O), which was an enormous intellectual leap for mankind. What if our plentiful liquid of life was glycerol ($CH_2OHCHOHCH_2OH$)? In terms of learning about the reality of elements, which led to the discovery of atoms, water acts almost like a simple ubiquitous tutorial. In other words, like learning to read using Dick and Jane instead of Shakespeare.

Freezing and Expanding: Every kid in science class learns that things expand when they get hot and they contract as they get cold. Water contracts as it gets colder too, but to a point, that point being about 4°C, then a sudden burst of expansion occurs around 0°C. This makes ice float. Liquid water must be readily available on the surface of the Earth for life to exist. Ice that sinks would not only hinder the biological processes at the bottom of a large body of water, but also accumulate as solid ice under the murky water far from the melting rays of the sun.

Specific Heat: It takes a lot of energy to heat water. Except for ammonia, water has the highest specific heat of any liquid. 70% of the planet's surface is water, which is a good thing for us since it helps regulate the Earth's temperature. Think of the hot sand on the beach on a hot day as compared to the cool water. What if water heated just as fast as sand? What would that mean for not only the Earth, but for our waterlogged bodies as we generate metabolic heat?!? We all know how sick we feel if our body temperature goes up just a few degrees.

Latent Heat of Evaporation: It takes a lot of heat to evaporate water and when it finally does evaporate it takes a lot of heat with it. Water is not only a remarkable cooling liquid for our bodies as sweat, but evaporation in tropical areas carries latent heat to colder climates which is released as it condenses. No other substance could absorb, store, transport and release so much heat.

Latent Heat of Fusion: An unusually high latent heat of fusion means that as water freezes in winter it releases the heat it absorbed the previous spring when it melted. Remember that the next time you complain a lake is freezing over. It would be even colder if water did not have this additional temperature stabilizing property.

Solvent Power: Water is a powerful solvent that is also not highly reactive like other solvents; it releases minerals from rocks without attacking biological entities and is also a great circulator of its precious cargo, being that it remains a flowing liquid at just the right temperatures. The expanding trick of water as it freezes opens the cracks and crevasses of rocks, releasing even more life-giving minerals.

High Surface Tension: Surpassed only by liquid mercury, the surface tension of water is curiously high. Water can rise to great heights and if trees and other large vegetation could be thankful, I'm sure they would be, since no extra effort is needed to pull the water up. There would be no large vegetation on Earth if not for this property, and what would that do to the planet's ecosystem? Additionally, clingy water will not just soak through to deep soil and underground streams. It grips to particles near the surface long enough for roots to soak it up.

Another Convenient Coincidence: The liquid of life just happens to exist in all three phases (solid, liquid, gas) within the same biological temperature range that carbon based life can occur.

Water is remarkably fine-tuned for life. One must accept the premise that all its properties are either a mindless coincidence or designed for a purpose; the purpose of life. Impartial reasoning accepts the principle that things that appear intelligently designed—are in fact intelligently designed. Things do not magically design themselves, no matter how much we would like them to and even some agnostic physicists are rediscovering and expressing this intellectual honesty.

"A common sense interpretation of the facts suggests that a super intellect has monkeyed with the physics, as well as the chemistry and biology, and that there are no blind forces worth speaking about in nature."

– Fred Hoyle

In his book, *Ten Universal Principles*, Fr. Spitzer recounts how, when he taught philosophy to university students, he would ask, "Are all opinions equally valid?"[39] Most students would answer yes, in the spirit of fairness and equality. Then Fr. Spitzer would use principles of reason like the ones mentioned above to demonstrate how some opinions are more valid than others. Catholicism is an all-encompassing worldview that can be examined by using classic, rational thought, and it all stands to reason. If God is the source of reason, then the reality of God and His Church will not violate the basic principles of reason.

Chapter 6

Convergent Paths
Two Sets of Data

So far, this commentary has been mostly a defense of Deism primarily via arguments from design and from morality, and still there is much more that can be said about these two topics. Sound conclusions come from considering *all* the relevant data, not just the data we like best. To put it another way, there is material data and immaterial data in the human condition; two paths of "data" that seem to almost provoke us into explaining their existence. They are like two rivers that converge and Catholicism naturally flows with and embraces both of them; this is even hinted at in the Catholic Creed where it says, "...all things visible and invisible."

The Path from Physical Reality

Of the several proofs for the existence of God offered by St. Thomas Aquinas, I identify most with the theory of contingency. I describe contingency like this. Every effect must have a cause and we cannot logically trace back causes to infinity. We can logically trace back to a "first cause", sometimes called an uncaused cause. A first cause, by necessity, would need to be simultaneously whole and non-composite, meaning totally self-sufficient and without parts. Nothing is needed for its existence, not even time or space, and nothing can be added or taken away including knowledge or power, or else it cannot be the first cause. From this premise flows that there can only be one first cause, which must encompass all knowledge, all power, all being, etc.

I struggled with the idea that we cannot logically trace back causes to infinity. I thought to myself, "Why not, just keep going backwards?" Then I read a good analogy for it in a book entitled, *How the Catholic Church Built Western Civilization* by Thomas E. Woods Jr.

Suppose you are at a deli counter to buy meat and you are told to first take a number. You are then told that you must take a number in order to take a number and this process of taking numbers to take the next will continue to infinity. You will realize that you will never reach the deli counter. You then notice that others have meat in their cart from the counter. You conclude that the processes of taking numbers must have ended at some point, at least for those with meat. It logically could not have continued to infinity as evident by the meat existing in the cart.[40]

Here's another way to think about contingency. Everything receives its existence from something else. You are here because your parents met. A valley exists because a river flowed there at some point. Try to imagine a universe where everything is a receiver of existence and nothing is a sender. If you showed someone from the far past a television set and explained that it receives signals and turns them into pictures and sound, the time traveler can logically conclude that there must somehow be a "sender" of the signal.

Isaac Newton and centuries of Aristotelian logic held to the assertion that our universe and past time were infinite. This created an apparent conflict with religion centuries ago. The Church taught and scripture supported that God created everything. Therefore there must be a beginning since the act of creating implies a starting point (see condemnations of 1277, #87).[41] But a true conflict between religion and science is always false because the truth is the truth. If we have a perceived conflict, it might be because the physical reality is not understood well enough or the spiritual reality is not understood well enough. It could also be a combination of both. Modern physics now explains how space and time do not go back to infinity, but have a certain beginning point. It's not well advertised that the Big Bang Theory was first proposed by a Roman Catholic Priest and scientist named Monsignor Georges Lemaître. This seemly unlikely connection between religion and science serves to emphasize the point that *both* science and religion lead to the truth. As far as infinite past time goes, it seems after all these centuries science is finally starting to catch up to Catholicism.

More Common Sense

Given a creation point and the complexity we observe in the physical world, the argument from design can be an intriguing argument for the existence of God, but it's also an intriguing way to explain unbiased reasoning. Imagine you were walking in a deep forest with a friend when you both stumbled upon a log cabin. You would naturally assume that something with intelligence created it, presumably a person or a group of people, even if there was no empirical evidence of a builder other than the cabin itself. Unless you had more evidence, you would probably *not* presume a specific builder by name, but the assumption of intelligence will become a base premise that is non-negotiable.

87

Now suppose your traveling companion said the cabin is just a result of the random forces of nature, matter and energy coming together over time to form the cabin. You would not only disagree, but perhaps also steer your friend toward some psychiatric help. Even if your friend could recite astonishing details about the forces of nature, matter and energy to prove his sanity, you might then conclude that he is so smart, he has become stupid. To accept your friend's conclusion would be more than just irrational; it would also be negligent.

Now, just begin to increase the physical size of the cabin. Suppose it was the size of a mountain. You would have the same conclusion about "intelligence". You will not presume the builder must specifically be Paul Bunyan, but the same impartial assumption about an intellect remains. Increase the size of the cabin to the size of planet Earth. You'd keep the same conclusion about intelligence, although you might drop the part about the source of it being human. Keep increasing the size of the cabin to the size of the universe—same conclusion. Now consider our minds, our bodies, our planet and the finely-tuned universe we live in that are all much more complex than a log cabin—same conclusion.

The science of the past took reason seriously with a premise like this; "We know the creator is intelligent, so we must go forward assuming the universe is intelligible." This is similar to our approach about the cabin. If you desired to learn more about the construction details, you would do so under the assertion that there is "thinking" behind it all. Today, many hold the backwards, upside down and non-negotiable premise of, "We know the universe is intelligible, so we must go forward assuming there is *no* intelligence behind it."

"It is truly glorious for a religion to have such unreasonable men as enemies."

– Blaise Pascal[42]

All this might sound very similar to Paley's watchmaker analogy, which may in turn remind us of some of the rebuttals offered by philosopher David Hume. For example, very complex self-order is observed in nature regularly like the process of snowflake generation from water molecules. This is true, but assuming intelligence behind it is still reasonable. Observing an application running on a computer may give the appearance that the computer is a self-ordered thing, but we know there is a programmer, not to mention a host of other precise, intelligent conditions needed for a computer to run.

Here is another; who designed the designer? If a well-ordered natural world requires a special designer, then this great designer requires an even greater designer and so on and so on ad infinitum. If we can accept a mysteriously self-ordered intelligence as an explanation for the natural world, why not just accept a mysteriously self-ordered natural world by itself? The problem is the reality we observe in the natural world; the data and the logic. Nothing in the natural world is really self-ordered. The order everything has is contingent upon the order of something else that came before it, until you trace back to some final reality that requires no other condition for its order. Why the need for a final reality? Why not just keep tracing conditions back to infinity? We have already discussed the unintelligibility of infinite past time, but an infinite succession of past conditions also presents us with a contradiction.

Premise #1: Infinity as applied to an accumulating succession is always more than can ever be achieved. It is unachievable.

Premise #2: For something to exist, all the conditions needed for its existence must be achieved.

Conclusion: Anything that exists cannot come from an infinite succession of conditions because it would depend upon an unachievable number of past conditions being fulfilled. To say it can is like saying the unachievable has been achieved, which is a contradiction. This is true for an infinite succession of intelligent designers as much as for anything else.[43]

The same kind of thinking and sizing process used for the cabin in the woods can also work in reverse. Suppose you observe a cabin the size of a single cell under a powerful microscope. To your astonishment, you not only observe the ordered structure of the building frame, but also indoor plumbing, electricity, a security system and a fully functioning HVAC system. Any reasonable person might ask, "Who built this?!?" Now consider a single living cell with a membrane, centrosome, cytoplasm, Golgi complex, lysosome, mitochondrion, nuclear membrane, nucleolus, nucleus, ribosome, rough ER, smooth ER and vacuole—all much more complex than any cabin. We reach the same conclusion.

"We know that even the simplest functioning cell is almost unfathomably complex, containing at least 250 genes and their corresponding proteins, each one extraordinarily difficult to produce randomly and none of which can function apart from the intricate structure of the cell."[44]

The evolutionary magic wand of natural selection and/or survival of the fittest cannot be used to explain how the first living thing came to be. The very first cell (or proto cell) had no parent(s), no genetic ancestors to evolve from; to say it came about through the random jostling of matter and energy might be a kin to saying a running car could come about through the random jostling of car parts. Whether a living cell or a running car, it's not just a matter of the right parts being in the right physical location; the parts need to be both integrated and interdependent for anything meaningful to happen. There is no reason for an alternator, an alternator belt and a battery to be carefully integrated together unless there was some intention behind it. It's the same with the parts of a living cell.

The famous Miller-Urey experiment offered an explanation for the origins of life, but not a convincing one. The experiment involved passing an electrical current through gaseous methane, ammonia, hydrogen and water (all assumed to be in Earth's early atmosphere). The result was the formation of some carbon-based compounds. I can see at least three problems with this as an explanation for the origins of life. First of all, carbon-based compounds are not living cells. Also, the experiment was not "mindless". The experiment demonstrates—rather ironically—how a precise set of intelligently designed conditions are necessary to form a "primordial soup". Lastly, there is no evidence of a primordial soup and atmosphere ever existing on Earth as it did in the Miller-Urey experiment.

"For materialists, in order for God not to exist, it was necessary for them to invent the soup."[45]

Consider an allegory about an intellectual blindness in regard to the origins of life. Imagine you are invited to a science laboratory for a special demonstration. When you arrive you see hundreds of small magnets strewn about the floor and strung together with some wire. A scientist then pulls an electrical switch. Suddenly, the magnets come together to form an elegant shape and the new creation begins to clean up the laboratory. When the last beaker is cleaned, dried and put way, the host scientist turns off the switch and all the magnets fall lifelessly to the floor. You are absolutely astonished and shout, "That's amazing!" The scientist replies, "Why? It's just a bunch of magnets." A similar attitude might be taken in regard to the first cell or cells on Earth, "It's just a bunch of amino acids."[46]

Such blindness finds its root in the sin of pride and the danger arises when we become more attached to our assumptions and over-generalizations than we are to reality. Our theories then become our idols. Idolatry at its root is basically worshiping things that are human-made. In demanding that the universe conform to our theories of randomness and mindlessness—because these are the easiest concepts for us to accept—we are transforming our theories about the universe into an idol.

A Word About Chance

Chance is not the cause of anything. If you win the lottery, it is not because of chance; it's because you picked the right numbers. If you roll two sixes with a pair of dice, luck was not the reason. You rolled two sixes because things like the force from your throw, gravity and the friction on the table caused the dice to fall a certain way. The "odds" are just an expression of probability, not an explanation of root cause.

Some interesting discussions can be had revolving around the odds of an anthropic universe (one that will allow the emergence of *any* life form) materializing by itself as a random occurrence. What are the odds of all the necessary physical constants being set precisely as they are? From here, what are the odds of a solar system and planet being formed arbitrarily producing an environment that can support the fragilities of life, while at the same time spinning around in a mindless universe that is so hostile to life. Once the environment is set, what are the chances of dead things becoming living things all by themselves and then evolving to become self-aware things like us who can sit around and wonder about it all?

91

Many analogies can be used to demonstrate something that might be physically possible, but can be called statistically *impossible*. A common one is a monkey and a keyboard. What are the odds of a monkey randomly typing at a keyboard and outputting a perfect transcript of Shakespeare's Hamlet? There are no laws of physics that will prevent the monkey from hitting all the right keys, but to think this will happen randomly is both unreasonable and irresponsible. If we did see it, would we say, "That's one lucky monkey!" or would we suspect an intelligent agent was influencing the monkey somehow?

But what if there are billions of monkeys typing on billions of keyboards. Eventually one monkey would do it, right? I don't think so. An experiment was conducted in 2002 at Plymouth University when several monkeys were left alone with a computer keyboard for a month to see what they would type for us to read. As you might expect, not a single intelligible word was typed in any language, just some random and repeating letters. Aside from hitting a few keys, the monkeys did other things to the keyboard, like bashing it with a rock, defecating on it and urinating on it.[47] If a billion monkeys had a billion computer keyboards, how many keyboards would be destroyed on day one? How many within the first year? How many within the first million years? The same random forces that might build up something favorable will also work to tear it down. I get a sense of this when dealing with some of the complex products and systems our company sells; random forces never help these things to integrate and maintain themselves, they only serve to breakdown the effortful design put into them. I think the same can be said when contemplating billions of planets or billions of universes.

What else is physically possible, but might be called statistically impossible? How about a game of pool? What are the odds of you breaking a pool rack only to find that the balls settled back down to reform the same exact triangle? Again, there is nothing in the laws of physics to stop it from happening, but it won't. If it did happen would you think it was an interesting coincidence or would you be spooked out of your mind?

Imagine winning the lottery—more than just once. What would be the odds of winning one thousand times in a row? There is nothing preventing you from picking all the right numbers every time, but you won't. If somebody won that often would you say, "lucky-bum" with a shrug of the shoulders, or would you say the game was rigged? The same is true with the remarkable fine-tuning observed in the universe. To think it can all happen randomly is irrational. Creation must be rigged in our favor so to speak.

So let's get back to contemplating infinite versus finite past time and why this matters when discussing chance. Things happening *before* the Big Bang obviously bring back discussions of infinite past time, space, matter and energy. This is a very helpful assumption to hold on to if we are to say there is no God because an infinite universe brings infinite possibilities, which makes the difficultly of improbability less difficult. This explains away the analogies of the monkey with the keyboard, the spooky pool rack and the mega lottery winner. Even with the Big Bang as the beginning of time, an infinite number of dimensions to our universe (a multiverse) will still bring back a discussion of infinite possibilities, but a multiverse cannot currently be verified through evidence. Of course, one might find it easier to believe in an infinite array of universes than an infinite deity, but this would rest on faith rather than observation.[48]

Intellectual honesty coupled with reason's responsibility construes that an intelligent unconditioned reality must have been the cause of every conditioned reality. In other words, there must be something beyond "the physical" which caused "the physical" and that "something" must be intelligent. Even with no absolute empirical proof and no faith, this becomes the most reasonable and responsible conclusion given all the data we have, including the new inputs from contemporary physics and philosophy.

The Path from Spiritual Reality

The God of faith is personal, defined by knowing and loving. The God as described by some philosophers is "The Supreme Being" and tends to be impersonal. In this view it seems strange that this Supreme Being should concern Himself with man and his pitiful little world, his cares or his sins. Oddly, this projects negative human characteristics of arrogance and aloofness onto the Supreme Being. We thereby imagine Him as a being that will not embrace everything and everyone, or worse yet, some kind of competitor.

By calling God "Father" and "Almighty", the Catholic Creed joins together a loving family concept that ties in more to spiritual reality and the cosmic power that connects more to physical reality. This expresses accurately a main point of the Christian image of God. It resolves the tension between absolute distance and absolute proximity, absolute being and direct kinship, the greatest and the least, and the first and the last. God is both-and, not either-or.[49]

Chapter two spoke at length about spiritual reality and it wasn't so much about angels, demons, ghosts or gods, but all about the Good, the Beautiful, the True and the meaning behind it all. A common and maybe unconscious reaction to such a claim is that spiritual realities are not really real; they are opinions relative to different individuals and cultures, or maybe human concepts that evolve over time. We went on to show that spiritual realities as well as physical realities are governed by both universal and unchangeable laws. The primary example used was objective morality, which is not part of the material world that can be quantified by the scientific method, but it is indeed real. If this was not so, no human action or behavior, no matter how heinous, could be objectively right or wrong, meaning it can only "be". The heinousness of it could only be subjective. Ethics then boils down to opinion.

I once ran across an individual who asked me this sweeping question...

"I'd like to learn more about this God. Are you suggesting that I read the Bible and follow the teachings of the Catholic Church in order to accomplish this? If so, why?"

Based on other comments from this individual the question may have been posed more sarcastically than sincerely, but whatever the case it certainly cuts to the chase. I also sensed that discussing the existence of God via the path from physical reality would not work out well with this individual. The physical path leads with the head in hopes that the heart will follow. The spiritual path proposed in the following leads more with the heart. Whether physical or spiritual, answering the question above does not start with the Bible or the Catholic Church, but there is a spiritual path that can assist us with the sometimes difficult journey from the heart to the head. The whole situation reminded me of portions of a book called *Jacobs ladder: 10 Steps to Truth* by Dr. Peter Kreeft.

Heart

Humans get passionate about transcendent things and I think we all know the difference between true passion and just a passing interest. We call it having "heart". Putting your heart into something implies having certain passion about it. Many are passionate about proper ethics, morals or justice (the Good). Others have their passion in art, literature, music, dance, theater, athleticism or nature (the Beautiful). Still others have a passion for technology, science, math, problem solving or discovery (the True). Many are willing to commit their entire lives to these kinds of things, even unto death. This is also how we know we are different than animals. Not even our closest animal relatives show evidence for having a true passion for "the Good", "the Beautiful" and "the True". But passion alone can ignite anything it touches. It's like blind power. This is why it is very dangerous to stop one's journey at passion. Osama bin Laden had passion for his cause. Imagine if his heart was driven by love instead of hate. Maybe we would call him Saint bin Laden someday?

Truth

Accepting absolute Truth is next on the journey. If you are truly passionate, it's not a big step to get from passion of the heart to accepting objective truth as something that is real. Holding truths to be self-evident, as the founders of this nation wrote, is different than a personal belief or opinion. If you are passionate in holding that genocide is wrong, you will not accept relativistic terms like "it's wrong for me" or "it's wrong in our culture" No, it is wrong— period. Just like a physical law, genocide being wrong is something universal for all cultures and unchangeable.

Meaning

Meaning is the next step. Once we consent to the existence of at least some objective truth, the acceptance of some meaning or purpose behind it all is not a far leap either. All people desire lasting happiness and the truths that we hold are meant to lead us to happiness. We use our heads and our hearts in the pursuit of that happiness that will eventually lead us to the meaning of life. It is also curious that humans would search for meaning. Why do we care so much?

The desire for meaning seems to suggest that a meaning exists, just like hunger suggests that food must exist and thirst suggests water exits. Even saying the universe has no meaning implies that meaning exists. How so? I think it is somewhat like the way counterfeit money would imply the existence of real money. In his book *Mere Christianity*, C.S. Lewis contemplates a universe with no light.[50] If light never came into existence, nothing would ever need eyes. If we had no eyes, the term "darkness" would have no meaning for us. It is the existence of light that allows us to understand the meaning of darkness. In a similar way, it is the meaning behind the universe that makes us understand what a lack of meaning would be. In other words, if there in fact was no meaning, we would never contemplate the question.

Now, if I have a desire for unicorns to exist, does that make them exist? If I desire to fly like a bird by flapping my arms, then I must have some ability to do so? If one said they truly desire a unicorn, is that really what they are after? What if the unicorn in question was obtained and turned out to be really smelly and mean and it bit you? Would you still desire the unicorn? I would suggest that wanting a fantasy creature to be real is actually a way to manifest the underlying desire for an irreducible thing of beauty and goodness or just beauty and goodness itself. How about the ability to flap your arms and fly? I would suggest the desire for true freedom is the irreducible good in this case.

One who looks to science to answer "why?" will not find "meaning"; they will find some answers in terms of cause or causes, which will in turn lead to more questions and more causes. Science tells us a lot about how something works, what it does and what physical attributes it has. The scientific method is frustrated, however, by questions related to meaning. Galileo hinted at this when he said, "Religion tells us how to go to heaven; science tells us how the heavens go."[51] As a result, a secular answer to the question, "What is the meaning of life?" might be, "We make our own meaning."

Fr. Joseph Ratzinger (future Pope Benedict XVI) addresses the question of "meaning" in the first chapter of his book, *Introduction to Christianity*; he describes meaning as the bread on which man subsists and how everyone knows the situation of "not being able to go on" in the midst of outward abundance. How many have plenty in terms of health, food, clothing and shelter, but live quiet (or not so quiet) lives of desperation. It's a problem related to "meaning".

Fr. Ratzinger then goes on about two kinds of thought. Calculating thought is concerned with "make-ability" and the physical side of reality. Reflective thought is concerned with "meaning" and the spiritual side. We need both to grasp all of reality and in an age in which calculating thought is celebrating amazing triumphs, we are all threatened by thoughtlessness, a flight from reflective thought.

Meaning is not manufactured from knowledge. We can study the physical attributes of an object for an eternity and never grasp its true meaning. Meaning, which is the ground on which we can stand and live cannot be made, but only received. Meaning that is self-made is in the last analysis—no meaning.[52] Consider a razor. If you think about it, we really don't understand what something like a razor is unless we know its meaning or its purpose. Imagine you were to stumble upon a razor, but didn't know what it was for. You will notice that it is very sharp and you might even cut yourself. Let's say you decide the purpose of the razor is to cut wood; what will happen? You will not cut wood very well and you will destroy the razor. Why? Because you did not know what the razor was really for. You did not know the intended purpose of its existence or the meaning behind it. Imagine bringing a person from the 1700's forward in time and sitting them in a car repair class during a lesson on the fuel injection system. The befuddled time traveler might stop and say, "Wait a minute. What's a car?!" From here we could explain that a car is a mode of transportation. The time traveler might then think of a horse and ask, "I have a horse for transportation. How is a car different than a horse?" We explain that a car is a machine, bigger than a horse, faster, can hold more people, etc. From here our guest student from the past would know the purpose for the cars' existence and how it relates to a horse. This kind of "knowing" and "relating" gives us a firm grip on the meaning behind any given thing.

Love

So what is the meaning of life, which will give us lasting happiness? If we are only physical beings, then it stands to reason that only physical things are needed to keep us happy. Outward abundance and physical pleasure should satisfy us fully and bring lasting happiness, but they don't. We seek more; we seek love; and love is not the same as "good feelings". If it were, we could say that taking drugs, which result in good feelings, is what true love is all about. So what kind of love are we looking for? It's unconditional, unselfish and sacrificial love. This kind of love involves more than feelings. It requires willing the good of the other, so it requires an act of the will or a choice. So love comes from an act of the will and it brings lasting happiness to everyone and is thus the meaning of life.

Part of the confirmation class I teach has a discussion about love; love as a choice. This brings blank stares of confusion from a group of young teens because everyone knows love is all about emotion; it's about how you "feel", but I ask them to think deeper. Previous classes discussed the soul as having two parts or two aspects; a will and an intellect. The action of our intellect is "to know" and the action of our will is "to love". So if love is an act of the will, then it is a choice, but how can someone internalize this; especially a teen?

Analogies are always helpful. Imagine you have met someone that you don't particularly like or are indifferent about. Now imagine you have made a conscious decision to spend time with that person, to talk with and get to know him or her, and to do things for that person. Now do all this consistently over time and you will discover feelings of love growing, but note that it all started with a choice.

Isn't this the general theme behind many, if not most of the movies we see? It could start with a young couple at the beginning of a film, who don't particularly care for each other, or even hate each other. They wind-up in an adventure together, get to know each other, and help each other to the point of maybe even saving one another's lives. What happens by the end of the movie? They end up getting married or something like that. I explain to my class that "love at first sight" can be a real feeling, but it should be given a more precise name. Call it "romantic infatuation at first sight" and remember that it is not true love.

Examples need not be only romantic. In the 1987 film *Planes, Trains and Automobiles*, Steve Martin plays Neal Page, an advertising executive desperately trying to get home in time for Thanksgiving. Neal meets Del Griffith, played by John Candy, a good hearted, but clumsy and overly-talkative salesman. They share a three-day odyssey of misadventures trying to get to Chicago from New York City. One could say that during most of the movie, Neal is annoyed by Del at best; hates him at worst. But as they spend time together, get to know each other and do things for each other, feelings of brother-ly-love develop between them by the end of the film.

Laws

Humans live in organized societies, which are guided according to certain principles, and those principles are reflected in the laws. If love is the meaning of life that will bring us lasting happiness, then the law should be love's servant and ally, not love's master and enemy. Good laws would support and be consistent with the natural law of love. Bad laws would undermine love and thus be unnatural.[53]

God

If there is sunlight, there must be a sun. There is always the physical path for the existence of God, like how the creation proves the Creator or the design proves the Designer. In the context of the spiritual or immaterial path, though, God is not a far leap of faith after accepting the natural law of love. If one has accepted objective truth or morals that are not sourced from human opinion, then there must be a truth giver of some sort. If love is from the will and is the meaning of life, there must be a first lover and a first "willer". If there is a natural or moral law that transcends us, there must be a "first cause" for it or a moral law-giver. A moral law-giver reasonably implies a loving personality with intelligence. Put this idea together with the "first cause" in the physical path and we are close to what Catholics would call God.[54]

An unconditioned, loving and intelligent "something" that transcends the natural world is the reasonable and responsible position to hold using reason alone, and we would all do well to ponder what a curious "something" that would be. Nothing mentioned so far definitively proves all that Catholic theology would say about God, but to say the universe and everything in it, from the stars in the sky to the love in your heart, is a mindless accident that magically happens by itself is truly wishful thinking for the non-believer who wishes to avoid the reality of things. In terms of believing in fairytales, the shoe was never so clearly on the other foot.

"Man does not explain himself to himself without the odd suspicion that he is missing something."[55]

— James V. Schall, S.J.

Chapter 7

The Rest of the Path
There's No Place Like Rome

How can we get from an unconditioned, loving and intelligent "something" that transcends the natural world to a reality that is all-powerful, all-knowing and all-good? Without a special degree in theology, I think these ideas can be reasoned through pretty well with basic logic given some of the premises already discussed.

In regard to all-powerful, I can remember reading the following passage in the compendium to Summa Theologica by St. Thomas Aquinas, "The more remote a potency is from act, the greater must be the power that reduces it to act."[56] With help from other Catholic thinkers that explain Aquinas, I can make sense of such a sentence. Rephrasing in more common language, it may read something like this: The less one has to make something potentially happen, the more power needed to make it actually happen. But what does this really mean?

Suppose you have a new car you wish to start. All that is needed is the key and the ability to turn the ignition or push a button; not very difficult. Now take away the gasoline. You now need the ability to get some gasoline, put it in the car, and then start it. More resources are needed. In a sense you might say that you need more "power". Now take away the battery as well. You'll need even more "power". The more that is taken away from the car, the more power needed to make it actually work. Taking away things to infinity becomes nothingness. Adding power to infinity becomes all-powerful. Imagine being left with nothing to work with. Not a single molecule, no space, no time, no energy, nothing. The only way you could make a car first exist, and then start it, is if you had infinite power. To create from nothing then, requires infinite power. All of this just to get one word in the Catholic Creed. The word "almighty" is not used simply because it sounds lofty and majestic. It describes, from logical necessity, the kind of power needed to bridge an infinite gap between potency and act.

What about all-knowing? God being omniscient could be described like this: There is nothing lacking in God's knowledge of His being which, being the cause of all that comes to exist, gives God knowledge of all existing things. Think of a person for this case. For a person to fully understand himself he would need to fully understand realities *outside* of himself. For example, how does a human hear? In the inner ear there are thousands of tiny hair cells. These hair cells change vibrations into electrical signals that are sent to the brain through the hearing nerve. How does that happen? For a person to have full knowledge of how he can hear, he we would need to fully understand the nature of all the electrochemical reactions and molecular structures involved. As questions are answered more questions arise and perfect intelligibility is simply never obtained. Additionally, if the intelligibility of a person depends on a reality outside himself, this demonstrates how that person is a conditioned reality. Since we have already said that God is an intelligent, *unconditioned* reality, then His knowledge of His own being cannot be restricted (or conditioned) in any way. And since He is the ground of all being, it doesn't seem like a far stretch to say God knows everything that is knowable or is "all-knowing".

Lastly, how can we explain God as all-good? If we hold the premise that God is "the first cause" of both physical and spiritual reality, then He is the source of all being. Think of the source of all being as if it were the source of all the light in a room. The light source gives 100% of the light. Other things in the room might block, diminish or disperse the light, but the source itself is always at 100%. So God as the source of all being would be at 100% or perfect being. If evil is only the deprivation of perfect being, then perfect being in the context of spiritual reality reasonably implies perfect goodness. Perfect goodness reasonably implies a God that is the all-loving source for the natural law of love.

If we believe an all-powerful, all-knowing and all-good God, what kind of logic flow could bring us to Catholicism? What's the rest of the path?

The Chasm

I think it starts with contemplating a chasm. We do not see God plainly or face to face. Catholic teaching holds that sin is the chasm that separates us from God, but this chasm is a simple step to reason through without any special Catholic teaching. If we have concluded that God must exist as all-powerful, all-knowing and all-good, then observation clearly shows us that we are separated from Him somehow. We also sense that the world is not as it should be. The world "not being as it should be" is essentially what sin is all about. Those who might say religion is about inventing a problem and then selling you on the solution are basically saying there is no such thing as sin and consequently, there is no problem. I'm okay and you're okay; everything about mankind is just as it should be. I think just one glance at the news headlines on any given day would be evidence to the contrary.

The Problem of Sin

The problem of sin can be expressed, and I think better understood, in terms of a cause-effect visual we sometimes use where I work. For any given deviation, whether a positive deviation (something good) or a negative deviation (something bad), there is always a cause or multiple causes and always an effect or multiple effects. Action directed to a cause is called corrective action and seeks to eliminate the cause. Action to an effect is called interim or adaptive action and seeks to limit the effect; more common names for action to the effect might be "workaround" or a "band-aid".[57]
See Figure 4.

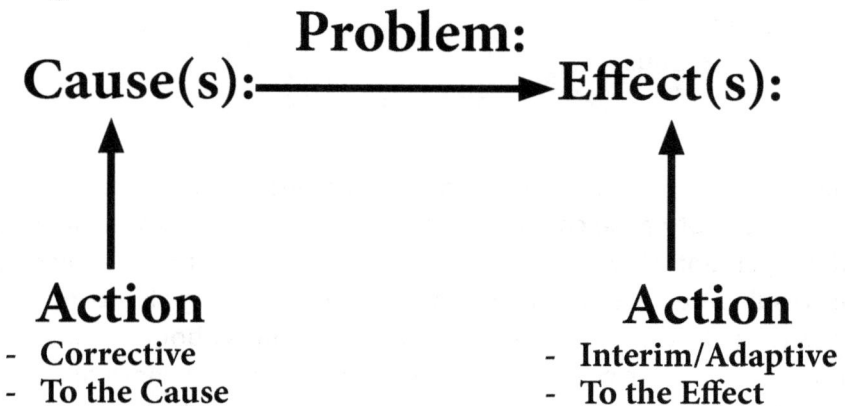

Figure 4

An everyday example is conveyed in Figure 5.

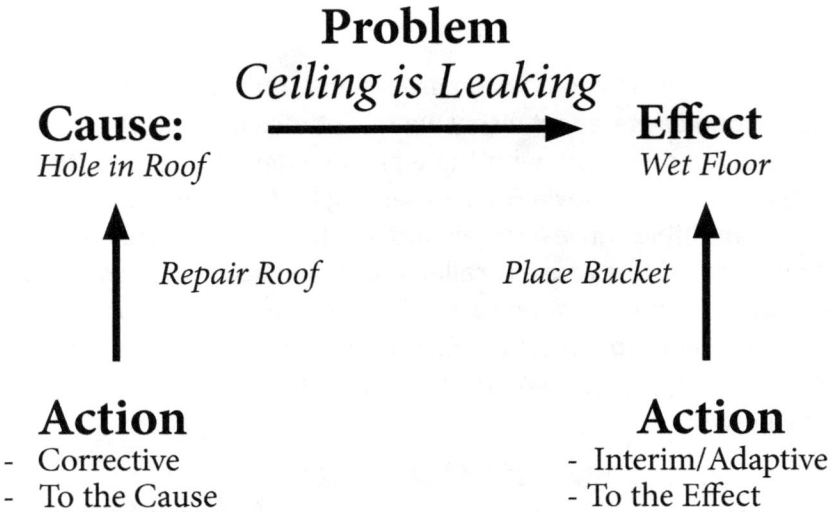

Problem
Ceiling is Leaking

Cause:
Hole in Roof ⟶ **Effect**
Wet Floor

Repair Roof   *Place Bucket*

Action
- Corrective
- To the Cause

Action
- Interim/Adaptive
- To the Effect

Figure 5

Sometimes it is vital to take action to the effect in order to buy time until the root-cause can be addressed. It's all part of good incident management. However, great confusion, lost time and lost resources result when action is taken to the effect, thinking all the while it was taken to the cause. Incident management is about putting out fires as quickly as possible. Problem management is more about defining a problem, being clear on cause vs. effect and in the end asking "What caused the cause?"

If you were to observe a hole in your roof, you'll naturally want to repair it quickly to avoid damage to your home. Once repaired, all is well and everyone is happy except a large raccoon that begins work on a new hole the very next night. Repairing the roof in this case can be viewed as an action to the effect whether you knew there was a raccoon involved or not. See Figure 6.

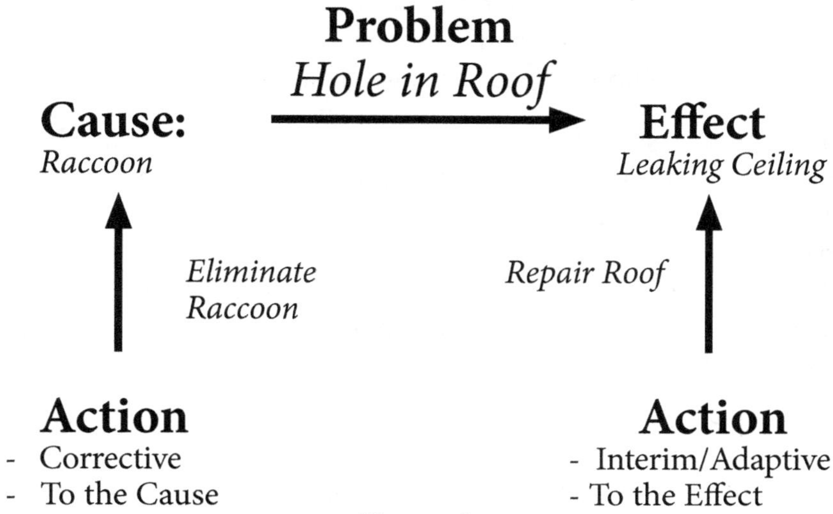

Problem
Hole in Roof

Cause:
Raccoon

→

Effect
Leaking Ceiling

↑ *Eliminate Raccoon*

↑ *Repair Roof*

Action
- Corrective
- To the Cause

Action
- Interim/Adaptive
- To the Effect

Figure 6

Defining a problem is especially difficult when confronted with multiple causes and multiple effects. Sin is the root of unhappiness. Whatever way the causes and the effects of sin are articulated we all take some kind of action, but regrettably, it is often action to the effects of sin. See Figure 7.

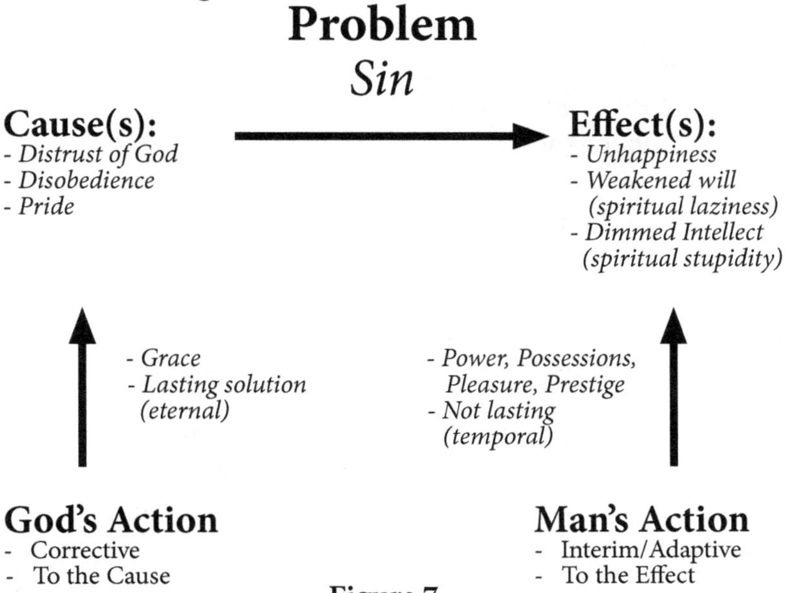

Problem
Sin

Cause(s):
- *Distrust of God*
- *Disobedience*
- *Pride*

→

Effect(s):
- *Unhappiness*
- *Weakened will (spiritual laziness)*
- *Dimmed Intellect (spiritual stupidity)*

↑ *- Grace*
- Lasting solution (eternal)

↑ *- Power, Possessions, Pleasure, Prestige*
- Not lasting (temporal)

God's Action
- Corrective
- To the Cause

Man's Action
- Interim/Adaptive
- To the Effect

Figure 7

God's Grace is the solution to the problem of sin. We seek pow-er, possessions, pleasure and prestige as temporal (or temporary) workarounds to unhappiness or dissatisfaction with life.

The solution is simple in one sense, but not so simple in another; similar to weight loss. If you burn more calories than you take in, you will lose weight; it's very simple. What could be simpler? But how difficult is it to lose weight with our natural tendency towards fatty food, our bad habits, hunger pains and the "culture of food" we live in? It's the same way with sin and we need God's Grace to overcome it.

Does God Care?

As a point of general reason, I think it can be said that creators tend to care about their creations, but we might ask why God would be concerned about any separation from us. Why would He care about our sins, our puny world and our puny lives? If we have said that God is all-loving then love itself is the reason, as Blaise Pascal said, "The heart has its reasons of which reason knows nothing."[58]

God has reached out to man and revealed Himself publicly, and in a big way, to both believers and non-believers when establishing the nation of Israel. The Hebrew people were few and weak, but broke out of bondage and survived for thousands of years even with many powerful nations wanting to destroy them. We read about these events in the Bible, but could we not argue that these stories are only myths and legends passed down from generation to gener-ation? As mentioned in chapter five, how can we know *anything* about our distant past aside from archaeological finds? History not only reveals the past, but also conceals it! When there were no re-cording devices and no structured print media, what did people do? Important things were eventually written down of course, but vital information was mostly passed on via the spoken word.

I think it is fair to judge the authenticity and value of whatever has been passed down through the ages by studying its fruit. The Jews received and passed on the greatest moral code in history (The 10 Commandments) which the world still lives by today. Far from a list of do's and don'ts from a divine dictator, the Commandments are spiritual laws of love from a divine Father that show us how to live. The boundaries of the law are like the boundaries of an embrace. If we live within this loving embrace we can deal with the problem of sin. If we push our way out of the embrace, we are left to take our own futile actions to the effects of sin. "If you would harken to my commandments, your peace would be like a river, your vindication like the waves of the sea" (Is 48:18).

The Jews also taught us that God is one, a person, a creator, eternal, perfect, faithful and loving. This notion of god or gods did not come from the Egyptians, Romans, Greeks or anyone else in history. The Jews taught us that God loves us and wants us to love Him and each other in return.[59] This fits with the meaning of life we have already concluded in the previous chapter.

The story of God and man can also be spoken of in terms of covenants. Simply put, Covenant theology is about God reaching out to bond with man over and over again and this certainly implies "caring". Covenant theology is not found in other religions and I don't think anything even comes close. For clarity, it should be emphasized that a covenant and a contract are different things that are worlds apart. A contract is a promise you make binding *your name*, often via a signature. It involves the exchange of goods or services, like building a house for example. A covenant is swearing an oath invoking *God's name*, and it involves an exchange of persons, like marriage. So a covenant carries much more weight in terms of blessings and curses.[60]

This is what many of the stories in the Bible are all about. In the Catholic view, the Bible is not a science book or even a history book; it's more of a story about a relationship between God and man, and a rather dysfunctional relationship at that. God repeatedly bonds with man through covenant mediators despite all the problems. God made Adam a covenant mediator in his role as husband for the intention of one holy couple that didn't turn out so well. Noah was a covenant mediator for one holy family that also had its problems. In fact, every covenant mediator of the Old Testament was less than stellar. Abram was next with one holy tribe and then came Moses as a covenant mediator for one holy nation. King David followed as the mediator for the Kingdom of Israel. Finally, Jesus came along as the perfect mediator between God and man in His role as High Priest, Prophet and King.[61]

There is no point in having a way if it cannot be known. The alternative is to say there is no certainty with God. Particular problems tend to have particular solutions. Since I deal with problem solving for a global company, I know there is often more than one solution to a problem; more than one way to skin a cat. When faced with a serious global situation, however, we standardize one global solution intended for everyone experiencing the problem. It stands to reason that if there is a God, He would also provide a global solution.

Christ

The Jews were expecting a savior to "make things right" and God went public once again in the person of Jesus. Although many Jews were expecting a political savior, a savior that can free us from sin through sacrificial love makes more sense in the logic of love we have been following. If sin is the chasm that separates us from God, then we are separated from the source of love. If we hold that love is the meaning of life as discussed in the previous chapter, it makes sense that we need to be freed from sin in order to travel properly on the journey from human passion all the way up to becoming an adopted son or daughter of God.

Jesus claimed to not only know the way the back to God, but to actually be "The Way" by making himself equal to God. Other religious figures like Buddha or Mohammad were not anticipated ahead of their birth and certainly did not make the radical claims or do the radical things that Jesus did. God went public in the person of Jesus through many public miracles and a public resurrection with many witnesses.

Making claims or doing things that implied you were equal to God would get you killed in the time and place where Jesus lived and even in some places today. You might be familiar with the trilemma offed by C.S. Lewis. Christ was either a liar who wanted to accomplish something great no matter what the cost, or He was a lunatic who was not God, but really did think He was God. Or He actually was who He said He was. [62] I think something similar could be said for the twelve Apostles and other followers of Jesus; they either passed on a bunch of lies, or a bunch of their delusions, or they actually gave an account of what really happened.

If the miracles in the New Testament are actually true, especially the Resurrection of Christ, I think the theories of lying and lunacy pretty much fade away. If there were no miracles and no Resurrection, we are left with a situation where thousands of Jews and gentiles simply and quickly walked away from their well-established culture and/or religion for loyalty to a man who died a disgraceful death in the eyes of any first century person. For a Jew, this breach with the faith of their fathers would not only mean expulsion from their community, but also an uncertain future for them and their families in the midst of a ruthless persecution. The gentiles that converted would have also been in the same boat.

But perhaps the trilemma is really quad-lemma? Maybe there is a fourth option; Jesus never made the claims or did the things as found in the New Testament. Maybe stories were exaggerated over time. Think of the game where you whisper a story in someone's ear and they in turn whisper it to someone else and this goes on and on. When the story gets back to you in a few minutes, it has changed. Imagine if this game went on for years or decades; the story could become utterly fantastic. Let's focus on rising from the dead in light of this fourth leg of "myth".

I See Dead People

Of all the miracles found in the New Testament, people rising from the dead must be the most fantastic. Even with today's medical marvels, someone getting up as good as new after being dead for days would certainly make some headlines. A resurrection would also be a difficult hoax to pull off even once, not to mention several times. Jesus raised the son of the widow in the town of Nain (Luke 7:11-15), the daughter of Jairus (Luke 8:41-42, 49-55) and Lazarus from the dead (John 11:1-44). St. Paul notes five hundred witnesses of the risen Christ (1 Corth 15:6). St. Peter raised Tabitha from the dead in the town of Joppa (Acts 9:36-41) and Eutychus was raised from the dead by Paul (Acts 20:9-12).

Think how much money a phony faith healer could make if he or she could hoax a resurrection? How famous would an illusionist or street magician become if he or she could do the same? Why have they not done so? I think it would be just too difficult to pull off. People know what death is in every age and take it very seriously. It reminds me of those who have claimed that the Apollo moon landing never happened; it was a government hoax. I find the moon landing hoax conspiracy theory unreasonable because too many key individuals would need to be in on the hoax for it to be true. They would all need to keep their stories straight about a very serious matter for a very long time. The same would be true for a series of resurrection hoaxes, especially a series of hoaxes with specific names, places and details given. The Christians had plenty of enemies back then who might act as today's political "fact checkers"; people who would be more than happy to seize upon the mistake of giving specifics to prove it was all a sham, but this never materialized.

But again, maybe the authors of the New Testament were not lying and were not insane, but were just writing down the legends and myths that were exaggerated by the early Christians. I don't see how a myth writer would end up with such specific names, places and details, but beyond that I think the myth theory runs into a serious problem with "time".

Some may still dispute the first-century date for the Gospels, but no one disputes that Paul's letters were written within the lifetime of eyewitnesses to Christ.[63] If so, there is not even one generation with which to build-up such a fantastic myth as the Resurrection, which was obviously indispensable to the early Christian faith as we read in 1 Corinthians 15:14, "And if Christ has not been raised, then empty [too] is our preaching; empty, too, your faith." Additionally, over five hundred eyewitnesses to the resurrected Christ are mentioned in 1 Corinthians 15:5-8. If we hold the premise that 1 Corinthians was written about 20 years after an alleged Resurrection and that the Resurrection never really happened, we can invent a modern day example to give us some perspective about the timing and scope of such an extravagant myth.

What if followers of Martin Luther King Jr. began spreading stories about him rising from the dead and ascending into heaven shortly after his assassination in 1968? Imagine all sorts of other miracles and fantastic stories were also circulated about him during his life on earth. Suppose photography and other recording devices had not been invented yet. Would thousands of people just accept these stories even if Dr. King's body went missing somehow? In addition to this, imagine if believing in this resurrection meant being ostracized from your community and risking ferocious persecution for both you and your family. Would people just go along with this fable without more compelling evidence or some other impetus?

Now imagine that letters were published around 1988 (20 years after the assassination) articulating how there were hundreds of eyewitness to the resurrected King, many of whom would have been still alive in 1988, and how his resurrection is now an essential part of a new and radically different religion. Is it reasonable to think that thousands of people would really give their lives to these myths? If yes, would not a rapid spread of this new religion trigger Christians and atheist alike to descend upon those poor delusional people and all the so-called "eyewitnesses" to discredit their claims or perhaps find that the eyewitnesses do not even exist?

If the Resurrection of Christ is a myth, then this type of scenario is where the logic leads.

That Just Doesn't Happen

A resurrection certainly makes for a riveting story, but is it reasonable? In the end what is reasonable or unreasonable depends on the base premises involved. If one firmly holds that there is no such thing as God, then there is not much point jumping right into a discussion about the Resurrection of Christ. Even if one believes in an all-powerful God that can do anything, the Resurrection may still be dismissed as not credible because "that just doesn't happen". The mentality that says "that just doesn't happen" is part of the reason for teaching analytical problem solving, which trains people to go wherever the data leads, and on occasion it leads us to places in spite of our intuition and our experience.

One of the case studies we review in the class I teach is the Apollo XIII disaster. Apollo XIII was well on its way to the moon when at fifty-four hours and fifty-two minutes into the flight the origin of that famous phrase was born; "Houston, we have a problem." The word "problem" is an overgeneralization; the first specific deviation reported to Houston was "Main Buss B undervolt". This meant that one of the two main power distribution panels for the command module had fallen off in electrical output. A "large bang" was another deviation reported at the same time as the first. A few minutes later another deviation was reported; Main Buss A undervolt. Apollo XIII was suddenly losing electrical power and no one knew why.

Engineers on the ground immediately began some incident management (action to the effect) by reducing electrical consumption on the ship. About thirteen minutes after reporting the first deviations more came in. There was a sudden loss of oxygen in one of the two main cryogenic oxygen tanks and a gradual loss of oxygen in the other (oxygen was used on the ship not only for breathing, but also to generate electricity. I'd imagine this was because batteries powerful enough for the ship would have been too heavy to take into space). The ship's crew also reported that the ship was "venting" something out into space. With the ship rapidly losing both electricity and oxygen 205,000 miles away from Earth the situation could hardly have been any more critical.

While putting contingencies in place to deal with the problem's effects, NASA engineers also began analytical problem solving to find the cause. This was done even though they had no possibility of amassing all the data they would have liked. After analyzing whatever relevant data was available, the number two oxygen tank suddenly bursting was a possible cause that explained all the observed deviations better than anything else suggested. There was one difficulty with this proposed root-cause. NASA engineers knew that their equipment was the best and safest ever invented. The very idea of a main oxygen tank just bursting in deep space was simply not credible; this is what their experience and intuition told them.

Faulty instrumentation or what we might call "bad data" was another proposed cause. [64] This idea may have made some people feel better. If true, it would mean that the gauges and alarms were just malfunctioning, so there was no immediate danger and the mission could probably continue. Although I've never dealt with a life and death situation, I can relate to the true cause of a complex and costly problem eluding us because it was counter intuitive; it flew in the face of our knowledge, experience and intuition. When this happens the natural tendency is to pick a theory you like better and then build-up assumptions until it fits all the available facts. Preferred possible causes tend to be *under* scrutinized, while unwelcome possible causes tend to be *over* scrutinized.

The cause was indeed a rupture of the number two cryogenic oxygen tank. This cause could have been easily dismissed because "that just doesn't happen", but this is where all the data led and the engineers were disciplined enough to go there. Clear-headed logic in a crisis saved the crew. Had the true cause remained unknown much longer, it would have delayed the planning to get the crew back home and there was no time to spare. What caused the cause? Nearly two weeks before the launch, the ground crew damaged the number two oxygen tank after using a non-standard de-tanking method in a demonstration. During the flight, a routine stirring of the tanks caused an electrical arc and subsequent explosion.[65]

If there were no oxygen tanks on board, one bursting would truly be impossible. Someone insisting that the tanks did not exist would first need to be shown otherwise. Once it is made clear that the tanks are actually there, one rupturing could be at least considered. I think the same can be said in regard to Christ, His followers and the Resurrection. Even if you believe in God you can still ask questions. Were they liars, lunatics, legends or speaking "Truth"? One could answer "I don't know", but those willing to believe a particular theory would do well to remember the purpose of the historical method and the Principle of Complete Explanation, both mentioned in chapter five.

Without being either gullible or cynical, which theory explains the most data given no possibility of amassing *all* the data you would like to have?

Got Three Words for You

All the homilies, sermons, writings, scripture and even all the movies and television shows about Jesus can be distilled down into three basic elements expressed in three words—Way, Truth and Life. These three words describe what mankind had lost just as precisely as a key fits a lock.[66]

A major point in question is how Jesus describes Himself as the way, the truth and the life using the curious phrase "I am". If someone were to say I have or I know the way, the truth and the life, we study what they have or what they know if we truly want to understand it. Who that person actually is would be of secondary importance if any importance at all. Consider an ordinary teacher. We may agree that the knowledge he or she is trying to convey in class is the primary concern. The person teaching is not the focus and a substitute teacher is possible to find. If someone were to say, however, I *am* the way, the truth and the life, then we must study who that person is. "I am" relates to "who" as knowing or having relates to "what". Christ does not simply give us the way, the truth and the life and then leave us to follow as best we can. He gives us himself because He is all three and there is no substitute.[67]

Way: As was already mentioned, there is a problem. There is a chasm. The way is closed. We live in a fallen world. We cannot see God face to face as we are. Jesus is the bridge that reaches across the chasm between God and man. Think of this as a road to salvation that was closed, but is now open for everyone to travel on. Once the way is open, how do we begin navigating it?

Truth: Once a road is open we don't just wander around it aimlessly like lost sheep hoping to get somewhere eventually. A road always has a direction and a way of traveling upon it. There are lines and boundaries and signs and lights to obey. There are other travelers to consider. We cannot understand the road if we do not understand the rules of the road. We need truth to guide us on the journey. So how can we know the truth as we travel? How about the Bible? That's a good start, but not a good end. The Bible will ultimately point to something else, "...the household of God, which is the church of the living God, the pillar and foundation of truth" (1 Tim 3:15). Of course this begs the question "Which church?" since there are so many and they all have different road rules.

Life: If Jesus is the life, and we wish to live, then He must live in us. The strength of man alone is not enough. Imagine you were to travel to another planet just as you are. Not only would you never be able to live there, but you would not even survive the journey. The journey would require many special systems, equipment and supplies to sustain your physical life. In the same way our souls cannot travel back to God unaided.[68] We need a supernatural life. This is where the Sacraments help us.[69]

- Baptism is the birth or beginning point of the supernatural life.

- We can receive daily nourishment for the journey via the Eucharist, which is none other than the Lord Himself as our food.

- Just like the body needs healing from sickness and injury on a long and difficult journey, our souls need healing from sin on our supernatural journey. The Lord gives us the sacrament of Reconciliation.

- The Journey is long. We need to grow and mature while we travel, so we are equipped with the Grace given at Confirmation.

- As we grow and mature in our supernatural life, we are responsible to help others along on this challenging voyage. A vocation like marriage or Holy Orders helps us to advance the entire Kingdom of God forward.

- There is even a special Grace near the end of our journey to help us finish well. The Anointing of the Sick.

"In three words *Way, Truth, Life,* Our Lord sums up what He is. In the same three words we may summarize what He did. He opened to men the way of salvation, gave them the truth by which they might know the way, and the life by which they might travel it."[70]

– Frank Sheed

What About the Bible Alone?

Is it possible to navigate the path from deism to Christianity using the Bible alone? Some time ago, I had a religious discussion with a co-worker that took on an unexpected twist. We were out at a local pub after the last day of a problem solving and decision making class. One of the members asked me, "So what else do you teach?" I responded, "Some technical product training and some religious education, specifically, confirmation class...I'm Catholic." He said inquisitively, "Really?" I said, "Really." He went on to tell me about how he gave his life to God a few years back and how it has completely changed his life; he described himself as a born again Christian.

As the discussion continued, he began to express his frustration with other Christians that do or teach things that are not found in the Bible. I set down my beer, sat up straight, took a breath and began to brace myself for what I knew would be next. I was expecting him to barrage me with a litany of things Catholics do or teach that are not (explicitly) found in the Bible, but it never came up. Instead he began to complain to me about other "born again" Christians.

He is a member of what Catholics would call a parish council over at his church. He complained that his pastor taught that any consumption of alcohol was sinful. One drink leads to two; two will lead to three, and so on. Therefore, starting this process with even one drink would be sinful even if you stopped at one. A Catholic might call this kind of reasoning inviting the "occasion of sin". There is some logic there, but my coworker had a big problem with this. The problem was not that he likes alcoholic drinks. His objection was, "that's not in the Bible".

On another occasion he attended a piano performance by his niece at a worship service at his brothers' non-denominational church. He began applauding after the performance, but immediately noticed that no one else was applauding. He also received some icy stares as he began to applaud. Afterwards, it was explained to him that during a worship service they only applaud for God. Applauding for others in church is taking away praise from God and is wrong. My colleague had a big problem with this also. Once again, the objection was "that's not in the Bible".

I thought to myself, "All Christian churches will do or teach things not specifically found in the Bible". What clear, real-world examples of how the teaching of Sola Scriptura (Bible alone) relentlessly affronts reason. Bible Christians do not actually use the bible alone; they use the bible along with whatever interpretations their leaders may have, and different interpretations result in different denominations as a natural consequence. I was going to tell him that using *only* the Bible is also something that is "not in the Bible", but I was afraid he might self-destruct right there in front of me.

Instead, I went on to talk about how scripture is subject to different interpretations and how the Catholic Church teaches that Jesus actually founded one, and only one, universal Church for everybody; a visible and authoritative Church that uses imperfect men, together with the Holy Spirit, to guide us in faith and morals. If there really is a God, He would provide a way for us to know what is true without deterioration from human interpretation. A good Father would not just leave a book behind for us to figure out; a good Father would not leave His children as orphans.

Of course, a good Bible Christian should be prepared to defend his or her beliefs inspired by 1 Peter 3:15, "Always be ready to give an explanation to anyone who asks you for a reason for your hope." But the Bible itself can be the trigger that informs you of a big problem—the Bible itself is not self-attesting to its own canon.

Why exactly would a non-Catholic Christian accept the present canon of biblical books as something other than human tradition?[71] Other writings like the Gospel of Thomas, the Gospel of Mary, the Didache, epistles of Barnabas and Ignatius (just to name a few) were written around the same time as what we find in the New Testament. Who has the authority to say what scripture is and what is not? It's not like St. Paul wrote his letters with special instructions saying, "Be very careful not to toss or lose this letter. One day it will be added to your scriptures so take good care of it!" Jesus never said, "This really smart guy named Paul will come long eventually and write a bunch of awesome letters, after I straighten him out a bit. Be sure to add his letters to the end of your Bibles." Ironically for other Christians, it is the authority of the Catholic Church that certifies the authority of the Bible.

Beyond the canon of scripture there are other doctrines firmly held by non-Catholic Christians that are not explicitly found in the Bible. Marriage should be defined as one man and one woman, right? You may be surprised to learn that there are no words in scripture that say a man cannot have more than one wife. In fact, when this question was posed to Martin Luther he said, "I confess that I cannot forbid a person to marry several wives, for it does not contradict scripture. If a man wishes to marry more than one wife, he should be asked whether he is satisfied in his conscience that he may do so in accordance with the word of God".[72]

How about the doctrine of the Trinity? There are verses in scripture that seem to hint that Jesus is not God, and the Holy Spirit could be seen as just an allegory for the power of God, not an actual third person. One could still use the old Arian-type arguments today. In the end, even Bible Christians fall back on an interpretive Christian tradition as a final authority.

"...I realized that my 'purely biblical' argument for Christianity was a series of neatly fashioned logic links attached to a hook hanging on a nail hammered firmly into...nothing."[73]

– Mark P. Shea

Even the meaning of individual words can be critical. In John 3:16 we read, "For God so loved the world that he gave his only Son, so that everyone who believes in him might not perish but might have eternal life." So what does it mean to believe? It seems that we need to be very clear about the precise meaning of this word. Is it just an intellectual or factual belief like believing the Earth is round or believing that two and two make four? James 2:19 says "You believe that God is one. You do well. Even the demons believe that and tremble." So if the demons can believe, should we believe the same way they do? Other verses seem to clearly link our belief to what we do, like in James 2:20-26. These verses link what Abraham did, in offering up his son, to his belief in God. (See also Romans 4:3 & Gal 3:6)

Sometimes it is helpful to think of opposites when trying to understand something. If we need to better understand the color white, it helps to study the color black. If we find out that black is the absence of visible light, it helps us to understand how white contains all the wavelengths of visible light at equal intensity. What is the opposite of belief? Is it disbelief? John 3:36 suggests that disobedience is the opposite of belief, "Whoever believes in the Son has eternal life, but whoever disobeys the Son will not see life, but the wrath of God remains upon him." Again, our belief seems to be linked to what we do, or don't do, as opposed to merely agreeing with something.[74]

This is not meant to be a biblical study on the concept of Christian Justification, but just an illustration of how static words on a page are subject to human interpretation. This is even alluded to in the Old Testament, "Ezra read clearly from the book of the law of God, interpreting it so that all could understand what was read" (Ne 8:8). When our nation's founding fathers wrote the Constitution, why did they bother to form a Supreme Court to interpret the Constitution? Did they not understand what they were writing? Did they not know how to express themselves? Could not future generations just read the words and understand what to believe and what to do in terms of governing a nation?

Many Christians may object to this reasoning about authority and still insist that there is only the Bible to guide us, but Jesus founded a Church, not a book. One might argue that the Bible is the living

Word of God, not dead words on paper, and that the true believer is guided by the Holy Spirit to the correct interpretation. In this case, all the disagreements among Christians and all the different denominations can be explained by people not listening to or misinterpreting the Holy Spirit. Of course, this triggers a serious question—who should I listen to if I do not understand and I cannot question the Holy Spirit directly? The Bible requires a teaching authority to go with it and Jesus didn't wait for us to invent a church of our own. We could all take a lesson in humility from an Ethiopian eunuch who lived long ago.

"Philip ran up and heard him reading Isaiah the prophet and said, 'Do you understand what you are reading?' He replied, 'How can I, unless someone instructs me?'" (Acts 8:30, 31).

What About Faith Alone?

I can remember the first time I read Philippians 2:12. "...work out your salvation with fear and trembling." The verse actually reminded me a lot of analytical problem solving if the word "salvation" were replaced with the word "solution." In terms of salvation, "work out" implies some sort of process, not something that is instantaneous, and "fear and trembling" reminds us that it's something that can be lost during said process. It seems St. Paul had a rather Catholic understanding of salvation. But how does one receive salvation and eternal life? Is it really by faith alone as some might claim?

Perhaps the Bible alone will clear this up. St. Peter's speech at Pentecost made it clear as we read in Acts 2:38. After receiving the Holy Spirit, Peter said to the crowd "Repent and declare Jesus Christ as your personal Lord and Savior and ask Him to come into your heart and you will receive salvation this very instant with no possibility of ever losing it." Well, that's not exactly what St. Peter said in the Bible, in fact, it is not written anywhere in the Bible.

So, are you saved? What must we do? What does the Bible teach?

Must you repent and be baptized?

"Repent and be baptized, every one of you, in the name of Jesus Christ for the forgiveness of your sins; and you will receive the gift of the Holy Spirit" (Acts 2:38).

How about just baptism alone?

"This prefigured baptism, which saves you now..." (1 Peter 3:21).

Belief in God alone?

"...whoever hears my word and believes in the one who sent me has eternal life and will not come to condemnation, but has passed from death to life" (John 5:24).

Words alone?

"By your words you will be acquitted, and by your words you will be condemned." (Mt 12:37) and "I tell you, everyone who acknowledges me before others the Son of Man will acknowledge before the angels of God" (Luke 12:8).

How about works alone?

"...who will repay everyone according to his works: eternal life to those who seek glory, honor, and immortality through perseverance in good works" (Romans 2:6, 7), "...those who have done good deeds to the resurrection of life, but those who have done wicked deeds to the resurrection of condemnation" (John 5:29), "Thus shall all the churches come to know that I am the searcher of hearts and minds and that I will give each of you what your works deserve"(Rev 2:23), and last, but certainly not least, "See how a person is justified by works and not by faith alone" (James 2:24).

Obedience alone?

"Whoever believes in the Son has eternal life, but whoever disobeys the Son will not see life, but the wrath of God remains upon him" (John 3:36) and "But if the wicked man turns away from all the sins he has committed, if he keeps all my statutes and does what is just and right, he shall surely live. He shall not die!" (Ezekiel 18:21).

Eating alone???

"Whoever eats my flesh and drinks my blood has eternal life..." (John 6:54).

Given all this, how can anyone claim—using the Bible alone—that salvation is by one thing alone? None of the above items can be dismissed as part of our salvation process, nor can any one item be emphasized at the cost of the others.[75]

In the last analysis, does the Bible really teach or do people teach? If it is people who teach then who should do it and by what authority? Would God provide for any such authority? The answer is found in the Church that teaches the fullness of faith as well as salvation in its fullness.

The Catholic Church

Jesus was tangible. He was historical, visible and authoritative, so it stands to reason that His Church would also be tangible, historical, visible and authoritative. Jesus authorized His Apostles and they in turn authorized their own successors. "There are two big reasons for believing the Church: to be sure to get the Bible right and to be sure to get Jesus right."[76] We need the authority of the Church when reason and the Bible aren't enough. Things like the Trinity or the cannon of scripture cannot come from reason alone and certainly cannot come from the Bible alone. All Church creeds are basically answers to heresies of the past.

If you reject the authority Christ established on earth, you obviously water-down or completely reject Catholicism along with other things, from what Christ actually taught, to what the Old Testament is about, to rejecting the idea of sin, which leaves you outside of reality—and that's where many people are today. "All roads lead to Rome; which is one reason why many people never get there."[77]

The Church is...

One: Undivided in belief and worship. In a free society we can believe and worship the way we want; the Church will continue to believe and worship the way *God* wants.

Holy: The Church is holy because it flows from the holiness of Christ, not from the holiness of any individual members at any point in history.

Catholic: The Church is catholic by its nature since catholic means universal. It is a global solution. The Church is for everyone in every nation. Would anything less make sense?

Apostolic: The Church is descendent from the original apostles. Jesus authorized His apostles and they authorized their own successors and this still goes on today. "So then you are no longer strangers and sojourners, but you are fellow citizens with the holy ones and members of the household built upon the foundation of the apostles and prophets, with Christ Jesus himself as the capstone" (Ephesians 2:19, 20).

It is the exception, not the rule, to find a strict materialist or atheist. Most people believe in a higher power of some kind—like "The Force", but it is often a faith that is devoid of reason, which results in blind superstition. Here is another quote I once ran across that sums it all up pretty well:

"There is a widespread idea today that it does not matter what our conception of God is like; how vague it is, how confused, even how distorted. 'We all worship the same God' has become almost a shrug of the shoulders, dismissing the responsibility of knowing God as he reveals himself to be, as if to know truly is no difference to us."[78]

– Caryll Houselander

Figure 8 illustrates "The Rest of the Path" as a logic flow chart.

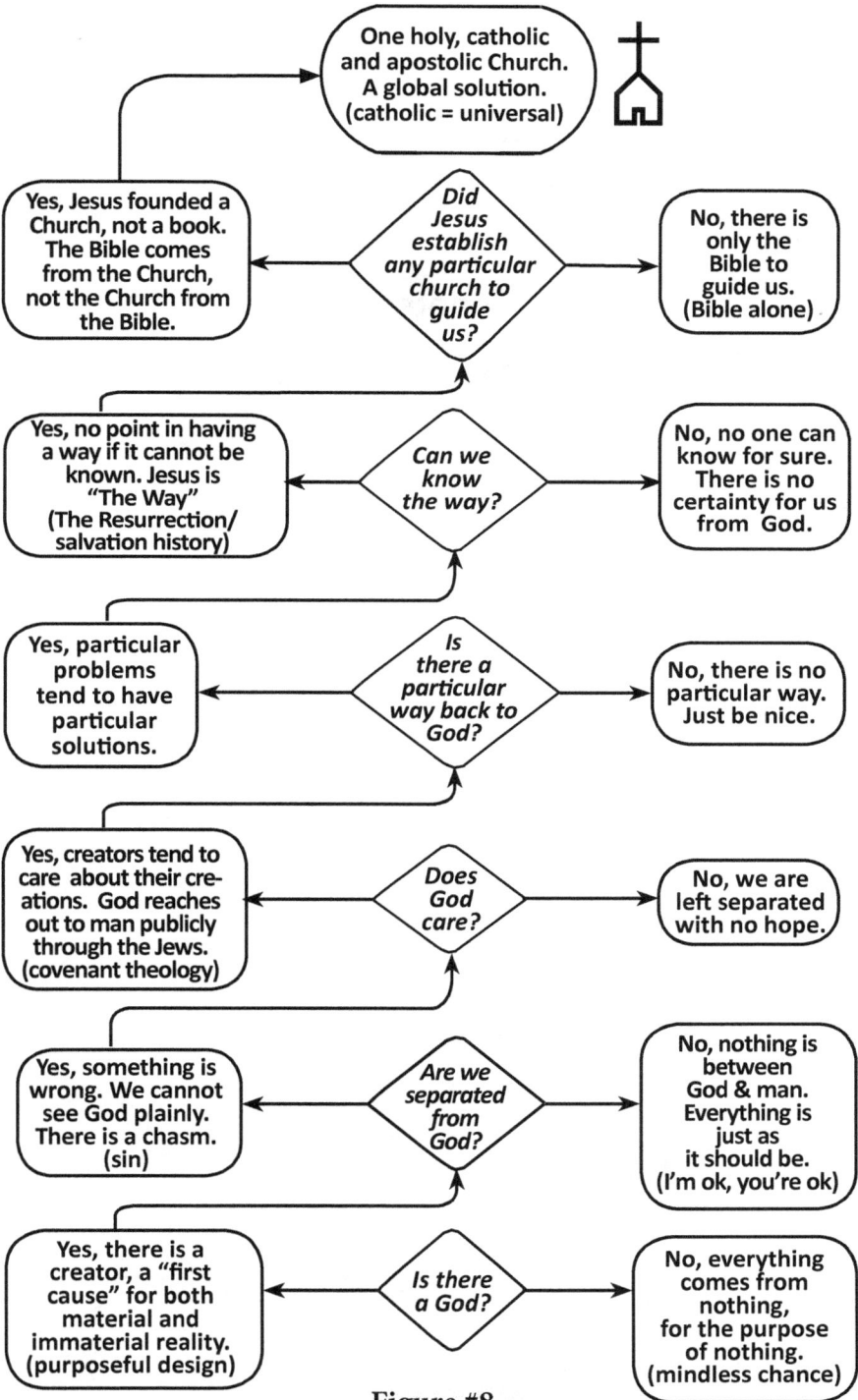

One holy, catholic and apostolic Church. A global solution. (catholic = universal)

Yes, Jesus founded a Church, not a book. The Bible comes from the Church, not the Church from the Bible.

Did Jesus establish any particular church to guide us?

No, there is only the Bible to guide us. (Bible alone)

Yes, no point in having a way if it cannot be known. Jesus is "The Way" (The Resurrection/ salvation history)

Can we know the way?

No, no one can know for sure. There is no certainty for us from God.

Yes, particular problems tend to have particular solutions.

Is there a particular way back to God?

No, there is no particular way. Just be nice.

Yes, creators tend to care about their creations. God reaches out to man publicly through the Jews. (covenant theology)

Does God care?

No, we are left separated with no hope.

Yes, something is wrong. We cannot see God plainly. There is a chasm. (sin)

Are we separated from God?

No, nothing is between God & man. Everything is just as it should be. (I'm ok, you're ok)

Yes, there is a creator, a "first cause" for both material and immaterial reality. (purposeful design)

Is there a God?

No, everything comes from nothing, for the purpose of nothing. (mindless chance)

Figure #8

Chapter 8

The Thorny Things

A consultant for our company once spoke at one of our group meetings about culture, wind, and paper airplanes. Corporate culture might refer to the beliefs and behaviors that determine how a company's employees and management interact with each other as well as with clients, vendors, consultants, etc. Culture can be subconscious, not clearly defined, and develops gradually over time from the cumulative traits of the people the company hires.

Imagine a paper airplane as a metaphor for an idea, methodology or policy ready to be launched within a company (like a new method of analytical problem solving for example). Imagine the culture of the company as the wind. If there is no wind at all the plane will go anywhere you like with some effort, but there is almost always some wind. If the wind is strong to your back when you launch the plane it has no difficulty going a very long way with very little effort. A plane thrown across the wind may start out in the right direction, but eventually turn and go wherever the wind goes. Launch the same plane into a strong wind to your face and the result is disastrous. Like a paper airplane that might fly back and poke you in the eye, the more an idea goes against a culture the more it will be viewed as a "thorny thing".

The same goes with how Catholic teaching is viewed in the wind of a given culture. Some things fly rather well. The Church teaches that racism is objectively wrong, that we should help those less fortunate than us, that it's wrong to rob banks and wrong to beat up old people, and I'm sure most would agree with these teachings. Some things don't fly so well, like the Doctrine of Just War, teaching on the death penalty and whether or not it's okay to water-board a terrorist. But most dissent from Catholic teaching involves something to do with human sexuality. Abortion, homosexuality, contraception, women's ordination, fornication, marriage, divorce and remarriage all have an aspect of sexuality to them.

The term "dissenting issues" is an overgeneralization and like with any good problem solving or decision making technique, overgeneralizations must first be separated and clarified before any clear discussion or action can be taken. Once more specific matters are listed, like those mentioned in the previous paragraph, they can be prioritized by considering the current and future impact of each one. It can be difficult to measure or quantify such things, but we can consider how many unjust wars we are currently involved with or about to jump into, how many people are executed each year and how many people are tortured or likely to be tortured in the future by the government. Now contrast this with all the effects of the dissenting sexual issues.

What are the current and future impacts of all the unwanted pregnancies and the resulting increase in poverty and single parent homes? How about the number of unborn children being killed and that will be killed in the future? Think of the impact from broken homes due to divorce? Ignorance and dissent about the true purpose of sex also brings us pornography, sexual addictions, molestation, sexually-transmitted diseases and marriage confusion. The amount of emotional pain due to fornication is probably not considered by most as something that will impact the rest of the culture in any significant way, but think of the huge number of people bonding and breaking up with different sexual partners over and over again and how this impacts their character? How then, does their character impact everyone else around them?

"Thinking means connecting things..."[79] Many, if not most, of the ills in our society can be traced back to sexual confusion or dissent. A game of theological "connect the dots" can help illustrate the connections between God, people, sex, and sin. We can start with the base premise that the devil hates God and if we are all made in the image and likeness of God, we can reasonably conclude that the devil must hate us.

A book called *Theology of the Body for Beginners* by Christopher West does a good job of explaining how people are created in the image and likeness of God. God is pure spirit and our souls are pure spirit. God has both a will and an intellect, as do we. The Holy Trinity is another way that is not so intuitive, but is the most profound. One way to think of God or the Trinity is as an eternal exchange of love. From the perfect and eternal exchange of love between the Father and the Son proceeds a third person called the Holy Spirit. How can that possibly be like us? In the union of Holy Matrimony, the love between a man and a woman generates a third person called a baby. The purpose of sexual desire is not only propagation, but also the very power to love as God loves.[80]

Now back to connecting the dots. If the devil hates us because we are like God and we are most "God-like" and mirror the Trinity in the covenant union of male and female, then the devil must hate *that* about us *more* than anything else. If this is true then it makes sense that a focus of attack on humanity would involve destroying families via the distortion of sex.[81]

You may know the acronym WWJD (What would Jesus do?) Stop and think for a moment about WWDD (What would the devil do?) In our culture, what would be the best way to tempt and ultimately destroy the lives of so-called "good people"? What would have the highest probability of success? Should you tempt them to rob a bank? You'd likely be wasting your time. How about something sexual? How about sexual temptation mixed in with some sexual confusion? Did God really say that's a sin? (see Gen 3:1) What's the harm? It's only natural. Does male and female really mean anything? Temptation coupled with confusion could do it and do it well!

Abortion

Anything sexual between consenting adults is now justified and sometimes glorified. We demand sex without babies. If unrestricted sex is something essential to a culture, then disposing of accidental babies is also essential. What other examples of killing innocent life is tolerated like this? For many, animals and even trees have more right to be alive than unborn babies.

God is the author of life, but to pro-choice secularists this is an unconvincing pro-life argument. The reflex rebuttals are, "You have no right to impose your religion on others." and the familiar "Separation of Church and State." At this point the dialog shuts down, but with many (if not all) of the thorny things, I find that secular arguments and reason tend to re-boot the discussion. When this issue is discussed using only secular logic one wonders how supposedly rational people can be *both* pro-choice *and* recognize science, reason and human rights all at the same time. One of the three must be "aborted". In fact, this is such a harsh contradiction; one can see a need for a diabolical force to help the pro-choice movement along; something to help generate a moral blind spot.

Scientifically, human life begins at conception as an objective and observable fact.[82] To say the first stage of one's life (or one's person-hood) begins at some other threshold of consciousness or viability is subjective; a matter of opinion. To declare something as important as this on something subjective is irrational (and devious), especially when an objective and observable beginning point clearly exists.

Pregnancy is a case where two human lives are physically inter-twined. When forced to decide if one life should be killed (perma-nently) vs. another life to be pregnant (temporarily), the reasonable course of action based on priority is to spare the life, because the right to be alive is the derivation of all other human rights and has the highest priority. Human rights are not a privilege conferred by government; they are every human being's entitlement by virtue of their humanity. The right to be alive is not contingent upon the choice of anyone else, not even a parent.

Once we get past religious objections and someone is shown how deviously subjective and unscientific the legal term of "non-person" is, the real issue of Human Rights can finally be addressed. Such discussions can immediately devolve into arguments via exception. "What about women and girls pregnant from rape and incest?" As if this was the main reason abortions are sought. "What about all the women about to die or be maimed because they are pregnant?" As if pro-life means choosing the life of the baby over the moth-er. In light of these objections we should ask ourselves if common law should really be based on exceptions. Even when rape/incest exceptions are proposed to those who lean pro-life, the objections still come. Women and girls might feel too distressed to tell anyone what happened and they should not be penalized; we need to be compassionate to women when they're in a crisis situation, so let's keep abortion "as is". What about the babies facing a pending abor-tion? Isn't that a crisis situation for them?

The "distress" objection mentioned seems to take this kind of exception fallacy to a new level. A small percentage of pregnancies are from rape or incest, and some small percentages of *those* wom-en are too distressed to report the crime, therefore let's continue the status quo. Some comparison logic about exceptions can be used once someone understands that an unborn baby is simply a person at the earliest stage of his or her life—nothing more and nothing less.

- Premise: Killing unborn children is wrong.

- Exception: Some women who become pregnant via rape or incest feel too distressed to report it and should not be penalized. We have to be compassionate to those in a crisis situation.

- Inference: Abortion should be legal whenever women feel they need to make that choice.

If this makes sense for abortion, it should make sense for other things too.

- Premise: Stealing is wrong.

- Exception: Some who are starving and feel too distressed to say how poor they are should not be penalized. We have to be compassionate to those in a crisis situation.

- Inference: It should be legal to steal food whenever you feel you need to make that choice.

- Premise: Killing is OK in self-defense.

- Exception: Some feel too distressed to report they were attacked and should not be penalized. We have to be compassionate to those in a crisis situation.

- Inference: It should be legal to kill whenever you feel you need to make that choice.

I could not say the number of times I've heard someone who is 100% pro-life called "extreme" in their abortion view, but I do not recall one time when someone 100% pro-choice was called "extreme" by the same person or group of people. Believing abortion should be *illegal* for anyone, for any reason, at any time is one view. Believing abortion should be *legal* for anyone, for any reason, at any time is another. In the logic of a spectrum, if one end is to be labeled extreme, the exact opposite end must also be extreme.

Let's consider "light" once again. The full presence of light (red, green, blue) is what we perceive as white. The absence of light is what we perceive as black. If we were to label the complete presence of light as "extreme white", we must then label a complete absence of light as "extreme black". So the next time you hear the Catholic stance on abortion labeled as "anti-choice extremism" recall that the exact opposite view and corresponding label would be "anti-life extremism".

Pro-Life or Social Justice[83]

There is a perceived dichotomy among Catholics to be either "pro-life" Catholics or "social justice" Catholics and it seems to come from the traditional political conservative and liberal extremes. Conservative Catholics might define themselves primarily as pro-life and place social justice in a secondary position because they feel if you are not alive all other rights don't matter. Liberal Catholics might be seen as social justice activists because Jesus and a vast array of saints worked for social justice, and therefore place their pro-life views in a secondary position. Maybe this is because the poor and oppressed are here now, whereas unborn babies aren't considered here yet.

Catholic teaching however, embraces both of those positions in a typical "both-and" fashion, so politically we sometimes choose a majority party and swallow the wrongs of that party in order to achieve the rights. This has the unfortunate effect of splitting Catholics into two separate and opposing camps.

Denying the right to life does undermine the U.S. Declaration of Independence's affirmation of Life, Liberty and the pursuit of happiness, which places Life in the primary position. All other rights are useless when life can be taken away by law. Therefore the inherent right to life is foundational. By any definition, social justice *assumes* the right to life. Social justice activists would never assert that the lives of the poor and oppressed should not be protected, so protecting life can be seen as a fight for the equality of all, born and unborn, therefore it is also social justice. The dichotomy then is false. Catholics should embrace both pro-life and social justice teachings and fight for the rights of all people.

Discussion about the rights of *all* people in the framework of Catholic "thorny things" could lead directly into a discussion about marriage. As with abortion, quoting the Bible or the Catechism of the Catholic Church might trigger the reflex rebuttals already mentioned. The "Adam and Eve, not Adam and *Steve*" argument doesn't go very far.

Much of the confusion about marriage today, even on only a secular level, can be related back to the System 1 (automatic/fast) thinking vs. System 2 (effortful/slow) thinking mentioned in chapters one and four. Drilling down with deliberate questioning is also important and the thinking and questioning can begin by asking, "Why is the government in the marriage business?" The automatic or "fast" answer might be to grant certain rights, like property rights, but we can and should continue to press with questioning and some effortful System 2 thinking.

Why does the government attempt to define marriage at all? Any definition requires limits to make one thing distinct from another. This is what makes a circle a circle and a square a square. They are both shapes, but they are not the same. If marriage means whatever you want, then it can mean anything, which makes it mean nothing. Some rational basis is needed for marriage to be coherent even on a secular level.

Remember that thinking means connecting things. What could link the things we associate with marriage? Why government? Why rights? Why two people? Why exclusive? Why permanent? Why sex? Why bother?

Does "love" make all the connections? If the rational basis for marriage was indeed love (or sexual attraction), it begs further questioning about why any government would care about who or how their citizens "love" and see some need to issue a license for it and grant privileges? How would the government define love? How could they distinguish between love and lust? Must it be only sexual love? Why limit love to only two people and why mutually exclusive?

What about "rights"? If marriage were only about property rights or civil rights, why would governing bodies discriminate (for centuries) against people *not* sexually attracted to each other, like close relatives? Shouldn't parents and their adult children be allowed to marry to obtain certain rights? If it were about rights, why bother with any specific number? Couldn't three or thirty people all agree to marry and share rights?

What about procreation? We should ask the same questions. Why government? Why rights? Why two people? Why exclusive? Why permanent? Why sex? Why bother? If government should be about the business of the common good, then marriage must be for something more than the gratification and happiness of only two individuals, more than accommodating a "special interest" and more than government acknowledgment for the sake of government acknowledgment.

Other than immigration, future citizens come about when one man and one woman get together. If this is the case, then it is in everyone's best interest that procreators come together and stay together as the best way to continue the human race; it's the indispensable foundation for any society. From here it logically follows that a government would want to set this type of union apart as *unique* from other types in order to incentivize it, protect it and grant certain rights for it. Only one male and one female are needed for procreation, so there is no reason for the government to give incentive for more than this; it only complicates things. This also explains why close relatives should not be allowed to marry; inbreeding tends to cause genetic defects.

Aligning the definition of marriage in accordance with the way humans reproduce isn't just some weird coincidence. People are getting very proficient at making assertions and demands about marriage, but not so skilled at asking and answering "why".

"It is not a pleasant task to call attention to the obvious. To make others appear to be shortsighted, let alone blind, may easily evoke resentment."[84]

– Fr. Stanley Jaki

Marriage Rights vs. Voting Rights

Why does the government grant any rights at all? Why would one set of rights be seen as unfair and another fair? To help answer the question it can be helpful to use part of a problem solving technique that compares what is perceived to be a problem to what is perceived to be OK. This also helps to determine if there is actually any problem at all.

No comparison is perfect, but comparing voting rights in the context of elections to marriage rights in the context of procreation comes eerily close. The granting of special rights normally implies some special responsibility with regard to said rights. If one is granted the right to vote or the right to marry, it follows that you should do something with that right for the common good.

So what can we say about voting rights? The base rationale for voting is to conduct elections. People given the right to vote are generally anticipated to actually vote, but no one will force them and no one will take away their right because of non-participation or if they have some physical or mental limitation. Not everyone is allowed to vote. There is an age limit because a serious responsibility is involved, and a unique status called citizenship is required. The French are not allowed to vote in a U.S. election and neither are the Chinese. This is not because of hatred toward the French and the Chinese; it is because they are not applicable to the situation.

The sought after outcome is a functional government. We all know that voting and elections do not guarantee a functional government, but if we have one, the elected members will strive for the common good and everyone wants that in the end.

So what can we say about marriage rights? If the base rationale for marriage (as far as the government would ever care) is procreation, then people given the right to marry would be generally anticipated to procreate, but no one would force them and no one would take away their right because of non-participation or if they have some physical or mental limitation. Not everyone is allowed to marry. There is an age limit because a serious responsibility is involved and a unique status of a male-female union would be required if we are to keep our procreative premise logical. Close relatives are not allowed to marry, and in some places still, homosexuals are not allowed to marry. This is not because of hatred toward close relatives and homosexuals; it is because they are not applicable to the situation.

The sought after outcome is a functional family. We all know that marriage and procreation does not guarantee functional families, but if we have them, the created members will strive for the common good and everyone wants that in the end. See Figure 9.

	Voting	Marriage
Supreme Objective	*Goodness Itself (God)* ↑	*Goodness Itself (God)* ↑
Higher Objective	*The Common Good* ↑	*The Common Good* ↑
Tangible Objective	*Functional Government* ↑	*Functional Families* ↑
Activity	*Elections* ↑	*Procreation* ↑
The Right	*To Vote*	*To Marry*

Figure 9

And then we get into all the "buts"...or what I would call "irrelevant data".

But any couple could adopt and raise a functional family. And any foreigners could vote in a U.S. election, possibly resulting in a functional government, so should we let them? Additionally, adoption is not procreation; it is about how to deal with children that are already here and have no one to care for them. If adoption is the same as procreation and justifies marriage, then why not let a father and his adult son get married? Why not a group of celibate nuns? Who's to say they could not raise adopted children just as well as anyone else?

What about surrogacy and impregnation? This is certainly procreation, but that's all it is. Any individual person or group of people can arrange it. If this is how to achieve functional families and the best way to continue the human race, then special marriage rights

134

would not be intrinsic for any couple whether heterosexual, homosexual or any other "-sexual".

But marriage rights have nothing whatsoever to do with procreation. Childless married couples prove this. If you give those who don't procreate the right to marry, you have to let any couple marry. Just like voting rights have nothing whatsoever to do with elections? People who don't vote prove this? If we give those who don't vote the right to vote, we need to let the citizens of other nations vote in U.S. elections?

But marriage is about love. And voting is about patriotism? Are we after some tangible objective for the common good or just granting rights for the sake of granting rights; rights for the personal contentment and satisfaction of individuals?

In the last analysis, if there were no elections, there would be no voting. If there were no procreation, there would be no marriage. Of course, if there were no procreation we would not be here to discuss it, but let's say humans reproduce asexually; would marriage exist at all? Seems silly, but think about that one.

Divorce

We've been watering down the logic behind marriage for decades. A slippery slope need not be as fast as the metaphor implies. A lava flow can be slower than 1km/hour, but will destroy everything in its path. The foundation for the marriage slope was laid by eroding the idea of "permanent". No fault divorce laws coincided with a message that marriage is a mere convenience—an institution that exists only for the personal happiness and pleasure of two individuals. For no fault divorce, it's basically enough to declare that a couple is no longer happy (irreconcilable differences). There is no need to "work things out". We can hardly blame the homosexual community for this. In the eyes of God however, divorce doesn't really exist. A couple may need to be legally parted in the case of abuse or other intolerable circumstance (see CCC, par. 2383), but once God joins a valid one-flesh-union, it exists. There is no way to make it stop existing. Consider your life. Once you are conceived, you exist. Nothing that happens down the road will change this.

Contraception

If no fault divorce is the foundation, artificial contraception/sterilization raised up the angle for the sliding slope of marriage. Homosexuals don't need contraceptives or sterilization so don't blame them. If marriage is for the personal happiness and pleasure of two individuals, then having children is obviously an unnecessary by-product.

Contraception blows apart the triune nature of marriage, sex and procreation, furthering the idea that marriage is about mutual gratification and sex is for anyone's pleasure, married or not. Once the rationale is fragmented, anyone can easily pick up the scattered pieces of marriage and reform them into something "else", something that does not reflect the image and likeness of God.

My wife and I help with the marriage ministry at our parish. One thing we do for the engaged couples is give a talk on sex and intimacy in marriage, which relates to the theology of the body, which relates to the image and likeness of God, which relates to the way God loves as we have discussed. Consider the Catholic wedding vows:

- Have you come here freely? God loves freely, so we should love freely. Love is an act of the will that cannot be forced. "No one takes it from me, but I lay it down (my life) on my own" (John 10:18).

- Will you honor each other as man and wife for the rest of your lives? God holds nothing back in loving us totally and permanently. "...he loved them to the end" (John 13:1). "And behold, I am with you always, until the end of the age" (Mt 28:20).

- Will you accept children lovingly from God? God's love is always fruitful and brings life. Marriage does the same. "...I came so that they might have life and have it more abundantly" (John 10:10). "Be fertile and multiply and fill the earth" (Gen 9:1).

Procreation is an indispensable part of marriage and the one flesh union should always be something totally self-giving that holds nothing back; it should be God-like. Catholics call this being "open to life". Whenever procreation is mentioned as part of marriage even on only a theological level, infertile couples are called on the carpet. If infertile couples can marry in the eyes of God and the Church, why can't gay couples? We must remember that an infertile male and female union is still of the same procreative "type" just like any male and female union.

Ponder a baseball analogy for a moment. A baseball team is orientated to winning baseball games. Even if they never win a game, no matter how much they try, they are still a baseball team and are always allowed on the baseball diamond. A football team also never wins a baseball game, but a football team is not relevant to winning baseball games and is not allowed on the baseball field, neither is a soccer team, or any other kind of team other than a baseball team.

My wife and I also practice NFP (Natural Family Planning). We have three children and used NFP to help achieve our first pregnancy; our son was born about eighteen months after the wedding. Not long after, we used NFP again to achieve our second pregnancy. Our first daughter was born twenty five months after our son. Around this time a co-worker said something to me (in jest).

- **Co-worker:** Nicely done; you have your boy and your girl. You're getting "fixed" now, right?

- **Me:** I'm not broken.

- **Co-worker:** Sounds like something is working a little too well.

- **Me:** I'll see a doctor about a medical procedure when something is wrong with me, not when things are normal.

We both laughed, but it brings up the point that we treat fertility much like a disease; we get prescriptions, have surgery and buy "gadgets" to stop it. If fertility is a gift designed by God, it would not be reasonable to treat it this way. Going beyond unreasonable, we have actually reached the point where *not* using artificial contraception is viewed as ignorant and irresponsible. My wife and I take the precise opposite view. Many are ignorant about natural law and irresponsible about sex, so what is the end result in terms of contraception? No birth and no control.

My wife and I also cover some of the Theology of the Body mentioned previously, and once couples hear the logic, they may think it's a nice theory that perhaps belongs in the heavens somewhere, but it's not practical for real people on Earth. We then get into the practical benefits of NFP, which have helped us.

More knowledge fosters better family planning:

It's not only for avoiding pregnancy and spacing children, but also achieving pregnancy. When a couple has trouble conceiving, one of the first things a doctor may do is have them try some aspects of NFP. You'll know if you're pregnant before a doctor can know. Many women miscarry without even knowing they were pregnant. We knew we were pregnant with our third child not long after conception and noticed some unusual signs, so my wife consulted with a doctor. A prescription to boost a hormone may have prevented the miscarriage of our youngest daughter.

It's "Green":

It's free and natural. In fact, there are those who use NFP simply because they prefer to do things naturally instead of artificially (no theological reason). It's really just common sense. Ironically, as we become more health conscious, we'll avoid natural things like fat, salt, sugar and pay extra for organic foods, but at the same time, gladly encourage women to pump themselves with artificial hormones via pills and patches.

Communication:

It fosters better communication between couples. NFP couples have very low divorce rates. Think about it; whether avoiding or achieving pregnancy, if you're going to be intimate with each other, you'll need to stay in "intimate" communication on a fairly regular basis.

It only gets better:

We experienced how a women's cycle can become more regular after having children, which makes NFP easier to do. As you start having children, spacing them out can become more and more important, so the woman's cycle becomes easier to read. God knows what he's doing when He designs something. Also, if avoiding pregnancy, the cycles of abstaining and being together mirror a natural dating-honeymoon cycle that continually breathes new life into a marriage.

From here we get into the two purposes of sex that should not be separated—babies and bonding. We use an analogy with food. Food has two purposes; nutrition and social bonding. Suppose you go to a party for pleasure and eat all the food you want, but you don't want all those calories, so you head over to the restroom afterwards and make yourself throw up. That's not the purpose of food! Now consider the other extreme, suppose a new one-a-day pill was invented which would provide all the nutrition you would ever need and you decided never to eat again. No restaurants, no party food, no dining with family and friends, nothing at holidays, no food ever. This would disorder your social life. We also explain how NFP is not like artificial contraception when avoiding pregnancy because you are using the gift of fertility the way God designed it. It's the difference between intentionally blocking something vs. just not participating in something.

Marriage is meant to be unitive, procreative, mutually-exclusive and permanent and none of these aspects can be intentionally separated. This is not true because the Catholic Church teaches it. The Catholic Church teaches it because it's true!

Euthanasia

Human sexuality is all about life, but euthanasia is all about death. Helping someone to kill him or herself is objectively wrong (see CCC par. 2277 and 2324). But how can it possibly be wrong under the secular "dogma of consent" covered in chapter three?

It's an overgeneralization, but I've always regarded "The Culture of Death" as simply employing death as "The Final Solution" to the problem of life. Could the right to die ultimately morph into an obligation to die through some basic secular logic? Of course, this is just another slippery slope argument and I was once told that slippery slope arguments are automatically invalid. If I let my kids play with matches, it will likely lead to a fire, which will lead to property damage, and someone getting hurt, and even someone dying, but this is just more nutty logic from a slippery slope. Regardless of what one might think of the metaphor, euthanasia could logically head down the following path and finally hit rock bottom via four distinct stages.

Stage 1: Voluntary – Passive
(Completely voluntary, but not applauded):
A small group of "enlightened" nations are completely entrenched into stage 1. This stage would have been unthinkable many years ago, but doctors may now lawfully help competent adults to kill themselves if they are terminally ill. Certainly, no one would be forced to do it, because that would be unthinkable. There should be no coercion either, since it's such a personal choice between pa-tients and their doctors.

Stage 2: Voluntary – Active
(Completely voluntary and encouraged):
We need to think of what is best, not only for ourselves, but for our immediate families and the common good of society. We live in a free country and no one can force you to do anything, but as a soci-ety we have an obligation to encourage what is "right" and promote the common welfare. The "right to die" can now slowly morph into the "obligation to die".

People are still free to smoke cigarettes today, but anti-smoking campaigns, legislation and taxation have done a good job of break-ing the will to smoke. The same can be done for those who insist on living for no good reason. Persistent social and financial pressure to do the "right thing" can break the will to live.

Stage 3: Mandatory – Passive
(Mostly voluntary with some exceptions):
As our population rapidly ages and the health care costs consume ever-larger proportions of government budgets, at least some legislation must be considered to help reduce the source of rising healthcare costs. Laws to guide the old and terminally ill through their final stage of life and their final obligation to the society just makes sense. Of course, such laws would be very limited in their scope and only apply to the most desperate cases. In fact, such laws are not likely to even be enforced much, like some immigration laws or gun laws today, so there is certainly no cause for alarm.

Stage 4: Mandatory – Active
(Mostly required with some exceptions):
Physician-assisted suicides need not be limited to only desperate pain. The very old, very sick and severely physically or mentally handicapped should all be considered for legal and mandatory euthanization once the quality of life has been properly assessed by professionals. Again, we must be mindful of the common good and do the "right thing" no matter how difficult it may seem. Why allow these poor people to suffer for no reason, even if they choose to suffer. Those in favor of such legislation will be called progressively "pro-health". Those opposed will be said to have a radical "anti-health" agenda.

As evidenced by abortion, we have been watering down the meaning and dignity of human life for decades and the stages above could take many decades more, but as a reminder, a slippery slope need not be as fast as the metaphor implies.

The Church and Women

The Church is clear about the ordination of only men to the priesthood (see CCC, par. 1577). Jesus and His followers chose men to be their successors. Some might say that is only because they were bound by the times; people in those days would never accept women as leaders. But if Jesus is Lord then He is not "bound" by anything unless He chooses to be and I don't think He cares so much what people think in terms of social norms. It seems to me that if He wanted women to be His successors it would have happened.

Men as priests also connects with the idea that being male or female is not only a physical reality, but also a spiritually reality. As a priest, the man acts in the person of Jesus offering the Eucharist to His Church, which is literally the body, blood, soul and divinity of Christ under the appearance of bread and wine. If Jesus is "The Life", then this giving and receiving of Jesus mirrors the giving and receiving that happens between a husband and his wife to bring about new life. No wonder the Catholic Church takes the definition of marriage so seriously.

If we view male and female as something only physical, we miss the greater reality, which leads to thinking a male-only priesthood is evidence of bigotry and a way to suppress woman. Once we have a better understanding what does the data show us? Is the Catholic Church an enemy of women or did the Catholic Church actually begin the idea of woman's liberation? In the book *How the Catholic Church Built Western Civilization*, by Thomas E. Woods, we can read some interesting points that are probably not taught in our public schools (or Catholic schools for that matter).[85]

- After the promiscuity of the ancient Romans, the early Church taught that fornication was wrong. Intimate relations were only for husband and wife restoring dignity to women and marriage in general.

- The Church also sanctified marriage elevating it to the level of a sacrament and prohibited divorce. This was a huge benefit to the women of the ancient world. Men could no longer just leave their wives with nothing to run off and marry another woman.

- Adultery, according to the Church was not confined to only a wife's infidelity, as the ancient world so often had it. The men were held equally accountable.

- The Catholic Church helped women gain autonomy. Women were allowed to form self-governing communities. Where in history were women able to run their own schools, convents, colleges, hospitals and orphanages outside Catholicism?

- So numerous were the women joining the Church in the early centuries and so numerous were the benefits they received, the Romans thought Christianity was a religion for women.

The supposed war on women is about people thinking rights are being taken away and taking away rights would be akin to losing freedom. But if we understand true freedom, then we understand that freedom is *not* being able to do what we want; freedom is being able to do what we ought.

The Church and Science

The Church and science might be a thorny subject for Catholics to handle, but it certainly need not be. In fact, it can be argued that the Church saved science.

Galileo seems to be the poster child for those who think the Church has suppressed science through the centuries. Galileo strongly supported Heliocentrism, which is the astronomical model in which the Earth and planets revolve around the sun and the sun is at the center of the solar system rather than the Earth. Around the same time the Catholic Church was sensitive to allegations by Protestants about the Church not having proper regard for the Bible. Certain Bible verses imply the earth did not move, but the sun did (see 1 Chron. 16:30 and Eccl. 1:5).

The Church actually had no problem with Heliocentrism being taught as a hypothesis and Galileo was free to do so. The problem came in when Galileo insisted on teaching and writing that it was fact without adequate evidence to support his belief. He also took the additional steps of playing theologian by saying that any scripture verses that were contrary to Heliocentrism needed to be reinterpreted. These two factors are what led to the charge of heresy.[86] In the end Galileo was right, which makes the Church look foolish, but ironically it was the Church that was insisting upon strict scientific proof.

Now back to how the Church saved science. Have you ever stopped to think about why modern science first arrived on the scene in Europe around the middle of the last millennium with scientists like Newton, Galileo, Copernicus, Descartes and Pascal? Why not from other great cultures of the past? Why do school children from China, Japan or the Middle East study what Europeans have done when learning about the origins of modern science? Why not study their own ancestors? This question is explored with piercing detail in a book called *The Savior of Science* by Fr. Stanley Jaki.

It's very understandable as to why some cultures would not be so concerned with the great "whys" of the physical universe if they were constantly struggling for food, water and shelter or continually fending off attacks from their neighbors. Who cares how the sun goes up and down every day if I'm just trying to stay alive every day?

But what about the people of cultures like ancient China, Japan, India, Egypt, Babylon, Assyria, Persia, Greece and Rome? They all lived in organized societies with infrastructure; they had long periods of peace and talented citizens. They were also not greatly influenced by one another, as if we could say the superstitions about nature spread from one culture to all the rest like a virus. Of course, they had their achievements, like gun powder, papermaking and fixed-type engraved printing all coming from China. How about the great architectural achievements of ancient Egypt, or the logic of the Greeks? But modern science never took root in any of these places. Why?

Like any good problem solving, one should compare the place of interest (like Europe) and the characteristic of interest (like the birth of modern science) to other places that lack that characteristic. From here we can look for distinctions. By their fruits you shall know them, provided that any scientific fruit is even looked for.

The great non-Judeo-Christian cultures of the past had their premises about nature, existence and the universe. Perhaps it was the belief in eternal cycles that left a hopeless feeling when at the bottom, or a sense of complacency when on top. How about the view of the universe as a kind of huge, wild animal whose dangerous irrationalities needed to be appeased by some kind of human ritual? Others kept a wall of division between celestial and terrestrial matter that could never be penetrated. Given these kinds of worldviews, it's easy to see why modern science could never take root. There also was no confidence in the abilities of a limited human mind to grasp the laws of nature, because nature was not subject to any rational mind or lawgiver that transcended it. King Brihadratha, the last ruler of the Mauryan dynasty, sums it up well for his culture as well as many others when he said "In the cycle of existence, I'm like a frog in a waterless well."[87] These kinds of mindsets seem to cry out for salvation.

So what was different about Europe? Fr. Jaki suggests that it was Christ that saved science from yet another "stillbirth" in Europe. The culture that grew out of Christendom was the distinction that provided the premises by which man could finally have a rational worldview. These premises came from Catholic doctrine.

Now this is a hard teaching; who could accept it? Didn't S.J. Gould get it right when he said, "Nothing is more dangerous than a dogmatic worldview—nothing more constraining, more blinding to innovation, more destructive of openness to novelty"? Isn't the scientific progress that we still build onto today the result of the

144

European enlightenment? Isn't this when men shook-off their pious little fairy tales about God or gods? This finally freed men to use logic and reason for the very first time to explain the world around them, right?

Well, the Greeks and other cultures were known for their logic, but science was stillborn in those places. Additionally, the famous forefathers of modern science like Newton, Galileo, Copernicus, Descartes and Pascal were all Christian. So if atheism or just raw logic does not explain the birth of modern science, what might explain it?

Fr. Jaki argues that salvation finally came for science because Christ and His Church built a Christian worldview with the following types of convictions:

- God is a rational being that is orderly and reliable; therefore, His creation is also rational, orderly and reliable.

- All matter, celestial and terrestrial, can be placed on the same basic level, since it was all created out of nothing (ex nilhilo). A pebble is no different than the Earth, the sun, the moon, or a cow in terms of being a created thing that can be studied and dissected.[88]

- Man is made in the image and likeness of God, so we can have confidence in human rationality to understand creation, because our intellect was fashioned by God in His own image.[89]

- Man can have full trust in a rational creator. This fosters the intellectual courage that can drive us to learn more about creation.[90]

Regrettably, this intellectual courage also leads men to the sin of pride. We can compare the sin of Eve in the book of Genesis to the sin of atheistic scientists today who view the world as only material. After being tempted by the serpent, Eve became "scientific", looking at the tree of life in a materialistic way. "The woman saw that the tree was good for food, pleasing to the eye, and desirable for gaining wisdom. So she took some of its fruit and ate it..." (Gen 3:6). The illicitness of the fruit and the tree was forgotten along with the Creator.[91]

Chapter 9

A Few Last Things

In a free society we get used to negotiating, settling, bargaining, haggling, meeting-in-the-middle and reaching across the aisle. These are great skills in the right context, but can hamper our acceptance of fixed spiritual laws in the framework of objective truth.

In the big-picture, looking at thousands of religious denominations in the world, we say that it is impossible for only one of them to actually be right. We try to negotiate all of these beliefs somehow. The truth is always somewhere in the middle; we must diligently search for the middle ground, but consider for a moment a horse race. Suppose there was a race with 20 horses and each horse owner was completely convinced, without a doubt, his horse would win. Must we then conclude that no single horse can possibly win? We'll need to settle on a 20-way tie somehow? Of course not! One horse will win.

If you are Catholic, you are on the right horse and this horse will ultimately win. If you're not Catholic, perhaps you should look this gift horse more closely in the mouth so to speak. The question then becomes, will you run the race with her? In the face of perhaps a new era of direct attacks on religious liberty due to all the "Thorny Things", understanding and clear thinking becomes especially imperative. Without clarity the cloud of confusion that billows from all the various religious denominations is quickly becoming society's second hand smoke.

Sincere Questioning

I remember having a metaphysical discussion with a secular friend about morality. The question in play was, "Does morality actually exist?" He answered, "Yes, but it's only a concept." I paused a moment and said, "Are you comfortable teaching your kids that?" I could see the doubt creeping into his eyes as he answered, "No."

Doubt is something we all can relate to until things are made clearer. From John the Baptist to the Apostles, to the greatest saints, to the most orthodox atheist, "doubt" is a part of our reality. "When they saw him, they worshiped, but they doubted" (Mt 28:17). "Are you the one who is to come, or should we look for another?" (Mt 11:3). Just as a believer can have reservations, the nonbeliever is troubled by doubts about his unbelief; about the reality he has made-up in his mind to explain the world as a self-contained whole.

There is no escape from the dilemma of being human, but perhaps this dilemma saves both sides from being too closed-up in their own worlds and prevents them from enjoying total satisfaction. The questioning that results could then become an avenue of communication. Belief has a bold "risk-leap" about it and posing heartfelt questions is a natural response[92]

Anyone sincerely and sanely probing for the Good, the Beautiful, and the True found in Catholicism will ask questions or raise objections in an open-ended way. As a cue, those looking to intelligently gather new information who are sincere, but not gullible, will tend to ask open-ended questions that start with words like "What, Where, When, How, Who, Why..." Think of how a doctor would ask questions if you were to complain that you are in pain. "Where does it hurt?" "When did it start?" "How would you describe the pain?"

Those who are cynical and wish to put you and your faith on trial may be more likely to ask closed questions, which are commonly used to help confirm things that one already suspects, and can begin with "Do, Have, Will, Can, Are, Is..." Think of a trial lawyer looking to get a quick yes or no answer. "Have you ever met the defendant before in your entire life?"

Consider the statement: **"Pink fairy armadillos eat stew."**

If one is predisposed against you, your way of thinking and your worldview, you may hear, "Are you serious?", "Have you ever seen pink fairy armadillo eating stew?", "Would any armadillo or fairy really sit around with a spoon eating some beef stew?", "Do you see how this is only a delusional fairytale?" If one is sincerely trying to understand, you may hear, "What do you mean by fairy?", "Why would any armadillo eat stew?" "What kind of stew are you referring to?"

I don't really know if pink fairy armadillos eat stew. I do know that a pink fairy armadillo is a real animal (look it up) and I suppose it might be possible that it would like to eat bits of meat or vegetable found in stew, but the point is this, any real understanding must begin with a heartfelt attempt to believe. You must first know what the idea would mean if it were actually true. This is part of the impetus of both problem solving and faith through reason.

Much of today's reasoning will happily accept certain ideas, like how our universe is highly intelligible, and at the same time, accept the idea that there *must* be no intelligence behind it. It's like accepting the idea of the ocean, but rejecting the idea of water. Intelligence at work behind creation implies a creator and also implies "intent". This would clearly risk a materialist's position. This kind of dimming down of the intellect is articulated well by the paradox, "We are smarter than we are".[93]

"We are smarter than we are" is meant to express the notion that our minds have evolved much faster than our bodies. The human brain appeared on the scene in a geological instant and it seems to be evolutionary excess in terms of only needing to survive and reproduce. In this context, evolutionary biologist S.J Gould is quoted as saying, "It does reinforce an ego that we do well to deflate."[94]

This "deflating" statement is not about the Christian virtue of humility; it's more about convincing you not to look any deeper than the material surface; meaning we should forcibly deflate that natural part of us that looks for spiritual truth. Paradoxes are normally meant to awaken the mind; in this case it is meant to suppress the mind. Our spiritual eye is meant to see further and deeper than the physical eye, but we are told to deflate the normal part of us that cries out "There must be more!" Should we shrink ourselves or should we continue to search for *all* things, seen and unseen?

Choosing to ignore the things unseen creates thinking gaps that divide us from God and from each other like a bottomless chasm, but Truth brings unity. In Luke 12:49-53 Jesus spoke of coming to "divide", but He came to divide us from whatever divides us from Him. He came to close the gaps. In order to actualize this however, we must make it our business to seek that which is greater than ourselves.

Beware the Boy Most of All

In the famous tale of *A Christmas Carol* we are given a ghostly warning about "our business". Mankind is our business, the common welfare, charity, mercy, forbearance and more.[95] Another ghost exclaims, "This boy is Ignorance. This girl is Want. Beware them both, and all of their degree, but most of all beware this boy, for on his brow I see that written which is Doom..."[96]

We are to help "the girl", but our doom seems to stem ultimately from "the boy". Why? Because what we know directs what we do. If God is Truth, then Truth should direct the will. If love is an act of the will, then to love or judge something, we need to know it. The primacy of the intellect is important in order to love and judge properly. In the end, you will not love a God you do not know—and you will not serve a God you do not love.

Our will reaches for what our understanding has seen. If we are ignorant of what is true, how will we direct our will? What will be our criterion for judging? Scripture gives us a subtle warning on the topic. "My people are ruined for lack of knowledge!" (Hosea 4:6). If we chose to ignore "the boy", then doom will engulf us all, because it all starts with ideas, and ideas have consequences. "Sow a thought and you reap an action; sow an act and you reap a habit; sow a habit and you reap a character; sow a character and you reap a destiny."[97] In the 25th chapter of the Gospel of Mathew we hear, "For I was hungry and you gave me food". This is certainly about physical food, but also about the spiritual work of mercy to feed the intellect. One can think of "Truth" as a kind of health food for the mind.

The seeds of God's image and likeness are in every person, so we have a natural hunger for truth/knowledge. Stop and contemplate "hunger" for a moment. What happens to people if they are hungry enough, for long enough? They'll eventually eat something; they'll eventually eat somewhere, but will it be good food or will it be garbage? Will they care where the food comes from as long as it gives some satisfaction? If we lazily accept anything that gives gratification we risk defaulting to our animalistic sensibilities and have the habit of replacing God with other masters since it seems to save us so much trouble. We all like to think of ourselves as independent thinkers, but people are like sheep and everyone eventually sits at the feet of a master. Who will feed your intellect about the Good, the Beautiful, the True and all the "Thorny Things"? Will you sit at the feet of Jesus through His Church or will it be some politician or political party, a celebrity or talk show host, a television evangelist, your favorite college professor, or will it simply be the always "infallible" majority? Who is your master? Whoever it is, be prepared to give an account for what you believe and what you say. "I tell you, on the day of judgment people will render an account for every careless word they speak" (Mt 12:36).

In the first chapter of John's Gospel we read about the two disciples of John the Baptist following Jesus and then asking Him "Where are you staying?" He replied "Come, and you will see." So they went and they saw (see John 1:38, 39). The same is true for us today. First you must ask, then you must "go", and only then will you "see". One who tries to observe from a distance experiences nothing. Only by sharing in the faith experiment does one actually have an experience; only by knocking is the door opened; only by asking can the intellect even begin to understand, and only he who asks shall receive.

Reason says it must be so. Faith says let it be so.

Endnotes

1 Meg Meeker, Strong Fathers, Strong Daughters (Washington, DC: Regnery Publishing, 2006) p. 55.

2 Daniel Kahneman, Thinking, Fast and Slow (New York: Farrar, Straus and Giroux, 2011) p. 20.

3 Kepner - Tregoe, KT Resolve

4 KT Resolve Flexible Instructor Guide: Opening Briefing (Princeton: Kepner - Tregoe, Inc., 2009) p. 18.

5 Frank Sheed, Theology for Beginners (Cincinnati: Servant Books, 1981) p. 186.

6 Sheed, Theology for Beginners, p. 185.

7 Mayo Clinic Staff, Mayo Clinic [Website], "Diseases and Conditions Lazy eye (amblyopia) Definition" (3 July 2013), Site address: http://www.mayoclinic.org/diseases-conditions/lazy-eye/basics/definition/con-20029771

8 Joseph Ratzinger, Introduction to Christianity (San Francisco: Ignatius, 2004), p. 73.

9 Karl A. Keiper, Wayseeker (Syracuse: Wayseeker, LLC, 2009), p. 226.

10 Joseph Pusateri, Two Catholic Men and a Blog [Website], "The logic of Moral Relativism" (30 December 2012), Site address: http://2catholicmen.blogspot.com/2012/12/the-logic-of-moral-relativism-part-one.html

11 G. K. Chesterton, Orthodoxy (New York: Doubleday, 2001), p. 13.

12 Chesterton, Orthodoxy, p. 7.

13 Chesterton, Orthodoxy, p. 24.

14 Saint Augustine, Confessions (New York: Barns & Noble Books, 2007), p. 5.

15 Chesterton, Orthodoxy, p. 13.

16 Taiichi Ohno, Toyota Global Site [Website], "Ask 'why' five times about every matter." (March, 2006, Site address: http://www.toyota-global.com/company/toyota_traditions/quality/mar_apr_2006.html

17 Bishop Robert Barron, Strange Notions [Website], "Why Goodness Depends on God", (10 January, 2014), Site adress: http://www.strangenotions.com/why-goodness-depends-on-god/

18 Kahneman, Thinking, Fast and Slow, p. 44.

19 Lynnclaire Dennis, Jytte Brender McNair and Louis H. Kauffman, The Mereon Matrix (Waltham, MA: Elsevier Publications Inc., 2013), p. 6.

20 Fr. Robert J. Spitzer, New Proofs for the Existence of God (Cambridge, U.K: Wm. B. Eerdmans Publishing Co., 2010), p. 110-111.

21 Spitzer, New Proofs for the Existence of God, pp. 110-111.

22 Spitzer, New Proofs for the Existence of God, pp. 111.

23 Spitzer, New Proofs for the Existence of God, pp. 111-112.

24 Saint Augustine, Confessions (New York, NY: Barns & Noble Books, 2007), p. 93.

25 George Weigel, Benedict XVI Light of the World, Foreword (San Francisco, CA: Ignatius Press, 2010), p. xi.

26 Fr. Robert J. Spitzer, Ten Universal Principles (San Francisco: Ignatius Press, 2011), p. 11.

27 Stephen Hawking and Leonard Mlodinow, The Grand Design (New York: Bantam Books, 2010), p. 180.

28 David Albert, New York Times [Website], "On the Origin of Everything", (23 March 2012), Site address: http://www.nytimes.com/2012/03/25/books/review/a-universe-from-nothing-by-lawrence-m-krauss.html?_r=2&

29 Augustine, Confessions, p. 93.

30 St. Thomas Aquinas, Aquinas's Shorter Summa (Manchester: Sophia Institute Press, 2002), p. 125.

31 Caryll Houselander, +1954, Magnificat, Vol. 17, No. 5, July 2015, pp. 131-132.

32 Spitzer, Ten Universal Principles, p. 14.

33 Ratzinger, Introduction to Christianity, p. 196.

34 Spitzer, Ten Universal Principles, p. 9.

34 Benjamin Walker and Jonathan Witt, A Meaningful World (Downers Grove: Intervarsity Press, 2006), pp. 130-131.

36 Walker and Witt, A Meaningful World, p. 133.

37 Walker and Witt, A Meaningful World, pp. 118, 183-189.

38 Walker and Witt, A Meaningful World, p. 155.

39 Spitzer, Ten Universal Principles, pp. 7-8.

40 Thomas E. Woods, How Catholic Church Built Western Civilization (Washington D.C: Regnery Publishing, Inc., 2005), 62-63

41 Woods, How Catholic Church Built Western Civilization, p. 91.

42 Peter Kreeft, Jacob's Ladder (San Francisco: Ignatius Press, 2013), p.16.

43 Spitzer, New Proofs for the Existence of God, pp. 180-181.

44 Walker and Witt, A Meaningful World, p. 201.

45 Walker and Witt, A Meaningful World, p. 209.

46 Walker and Witt, A Meaningful World, p. 217.

47 Walker and Witt, A Meaningful World, pp. 31-32.

48 Spitzer, New Proofs for the Existence of God, p. 5.

49 Ratzinger, Introduction to Christianity, pp. 148-149.

50 C.S. Lewis, Mere Christianity (New York: HarperCollins Publishers, 2000), p. 39.

51 Gregory S. Cootsona, Creation and Last Things (Louisville: Geneva Press, 2002), p. 28.

52 Ratzinger, Introduction to Christianity, pp. 71-73.

53 Kreeft, Jacob's Ladder, pp. 70-71.

54 Kreeft, Jacob's Ladder, p. 87.

55 James V. Schall, S.J., The Catholic Thing [Website], "Credo", (1 April 2014), Site address: http://www.thecatholicthing.org/2014/04/01/credo-4/

56 St. Thomas Aquinas, Aquinas's Shorter Summa (Manchester: Sophia Institute Press, 2002), p. 65.

57 KT Resolve Flexible Instructor Guide: Problem Analysis Techniques (Princeton: Kepner - Tregoe, Inc., 2009) p. 22.

58 Robert C. Solomon and Kathleen M. Higgins, The Big Questions (Belmont: Wadsworth Cengage Learning, 2014), p. 195.

59 Peter Kreeft, Jacob's Ladder (San Francisco: Ignatius Press, 2013), p. 95.

60 Scott Hahn, A Father Who Keeps His Promises (Beacon Publishing, 1998) p. 24.

61 Hahn, A Father Who Keeps His Promises, p. 35.

62 C. S. Lewis, Mere Christianity, (Broadway: HarporCollins Publishers, 2001), p. 52.

63 Arnold Lunn, The Third Day, (El Cajon: Catholic Answers Press, 2014), pp. 120, 145.

64 Jim Lovell and Jeffrey Kluger, Lost Moon, (New York: Houghton Mifflin Company, 1994), p. 96.

65 Charles H. Kepner and Benjamin B. Trego, The New Rational Manager (Princeton: Princeton Research Press, 2006), pp. 57-60.

66 Frank Sheed, Map of Life (San Francisco: Ignatius Press, 1994), p. 45.

67 Sheed, Map of Life, pp. 45-46.

68 Frank Sheed, Theology for Beginners (Cincinnati: Servant Books, 1981), p. 67.

69 Sheed, Map of Life, p. 121.

70 Frank Sheed, Theology and Sanity, (San Francisco: Ignatius Press, 1978) p. 255.

71 Mark P. Shea, By What Authority?, (Huntington: Our Sunday Visitor Publishing Division, 1996), p 55

72 Shea, By What Authority?, pp. 101-102.

73 Shea, By What Authority?, p. 55.

74 Stephen K. Ray, "Born Again? Faith Alone?," (Lighthouse Catholic Media, c. 2013), Compact Disc Tracks 7-8.

75 Stephen K. Ray, Crossing the Tiber (San Francisco: Ignatius Press, 1997), p. 100.

76 Kreeft, Jacob's ladder, p. 131.

77 G. K. Chesterton, Orthodoxy (New York, NY: Doubleday, 2001), p. 84.

78 Caryll Houselander, The Mother of Christ, (London: Sheed and Ward, 1978), p. 48.

79 G. K. Chesterton, Orthodoxy (New York: Doubleday, 2001), p. 31.

80 Christopher West, Theology of the Body for Beginners (West Chester: Ascension Press, 2004), pp. 27-29.

81 Christopher West, Theology of the Body for Beginners, p. 12.

82 Sarah Terzo, Lifenews.com [Website], "41 Quotes From Medical Textbooks Prove Human Life Begins at Conception" (8 January 2015), Site address: http://www.lifenews.com/2015/01/08/41-quotes-from-medical-textbooks-prove-human-life-begins-at-conception/

83 Joseph Pusateri, Two Catholic Men and a Blog [Website], "Pro Life or Social Justice" (22 October 2011), Site address: http://2catholicmen.blogspot.com/search/label/Social%20Justice

84 Stanley L. Jaki, A Mind's Matter (Grand Rapids: William B. Eerdmans Publishing Co., 2002), p .52.

85 Woods, How Catholic Church Built Western Civilization, pp. 211-213.

86 Woods, How Catholic Church Built Western Civilization, pp. 69-74

87 Stanley L. Jaki, The Savior of Science (Grand Rapids: William B. Eerdmans Publishing Co., 2000), p. 28.

88 Jaki, The Savior of Science, p. 75.

89 Jaki, The Savior of Science, p. 96.

90 Jaki, The Savior of Science, p. 43.

91 Jaki, The Savior of Science, p. 198.

92 Ratzinger, Introduction to Christianity, pp. 45, 47, 52, 80.

93 Jaki, The Savior of Science, p. 164.

94 Jaki, The Savior of Science, p. 165.

95 Charles Dickens, A Christmas Carol, (New York: Barnes & Nobal Books, 2003), p. 28.

96 Dickens, A Christmas Carol, p. 84.

97 Charles A. Fowler, Biblical Truths for Men (Innovo Publishing, LLC, 2014), p. 115.

www.ingramcontent.com/pod-product-compliance
Lightning Source LLC
Chambersburg PA
CBHW060256050426
42448CB00009B/1657